Real World
Colouring Book
For Advanced Users & Adults

50 Images

Created From Real Life Photos
For You To Colour As You Please.

ISBN 978-0-359-97226-5
90000
9 780359 972265

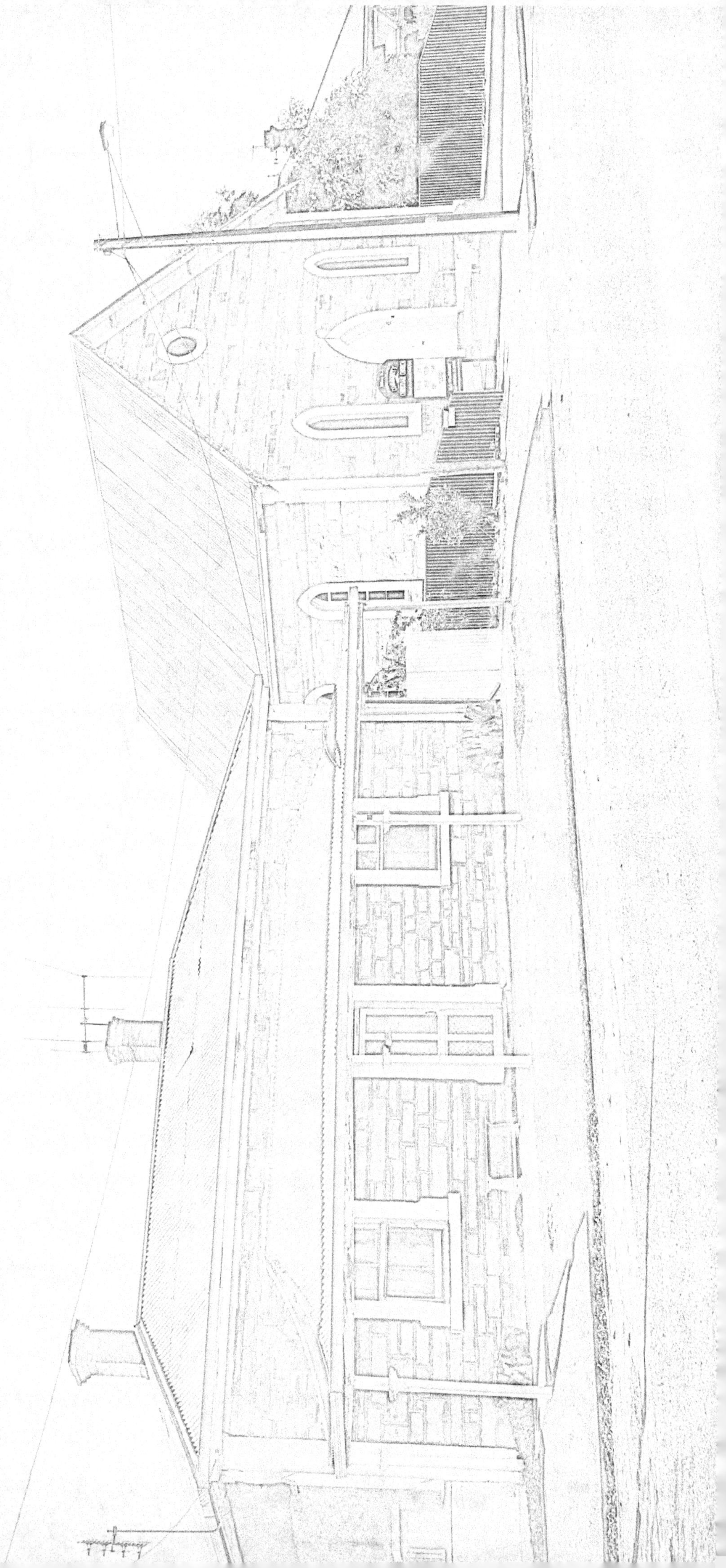

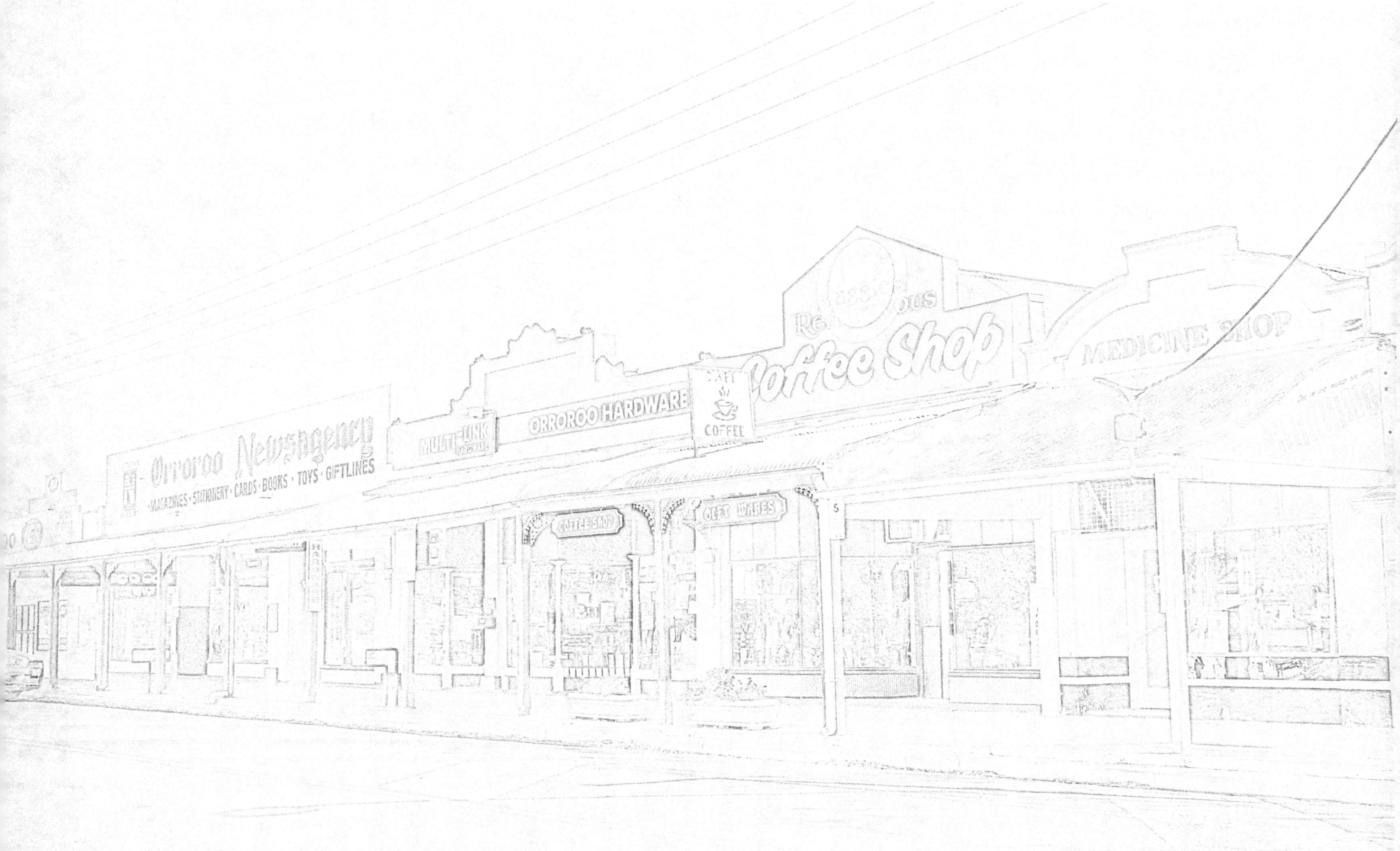
Orroroo Newsagency
MAGAZINES · STATIONERY · CARDS · BOOKS · TOYS · GIFTLINES
ORROROO HARDWARE
CAFE
COFFEE
Coffee Shop
MEDICINE SHOP
COFFEE SHOP

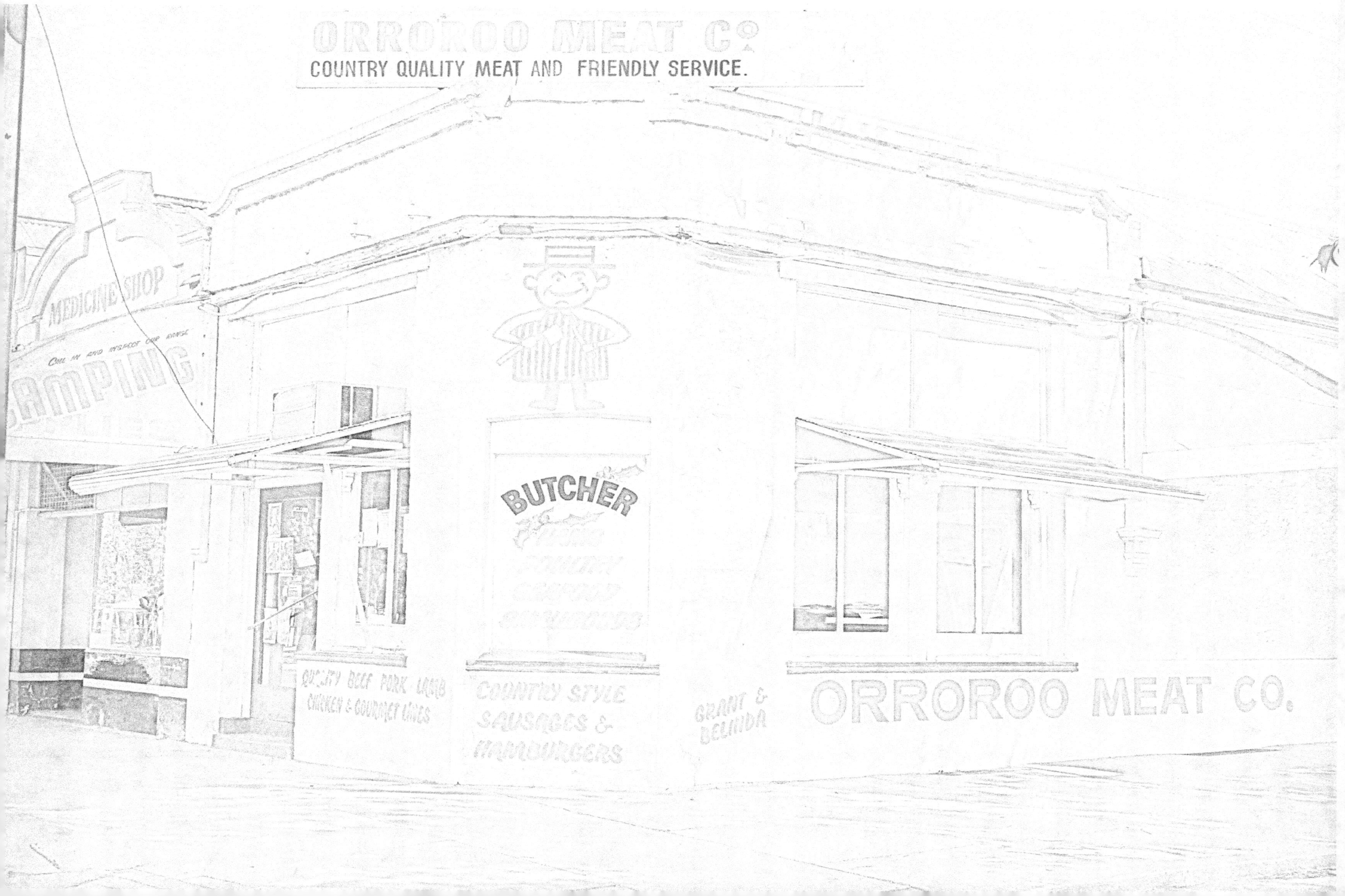
ORROROO MEAT Co
COUNTRY QUALITY MEAT AND FRIENDLY SERVICE.
MEDICINE SHOP
BUTCHER
QUALITY BEEF PORK LAMB
CHICKEN & GOURMET LINES
COUNTRY STYLE
SAUSAGES &
HAMBURGERS
GRANT &
BELINDA
ORROROO MEAT CO.

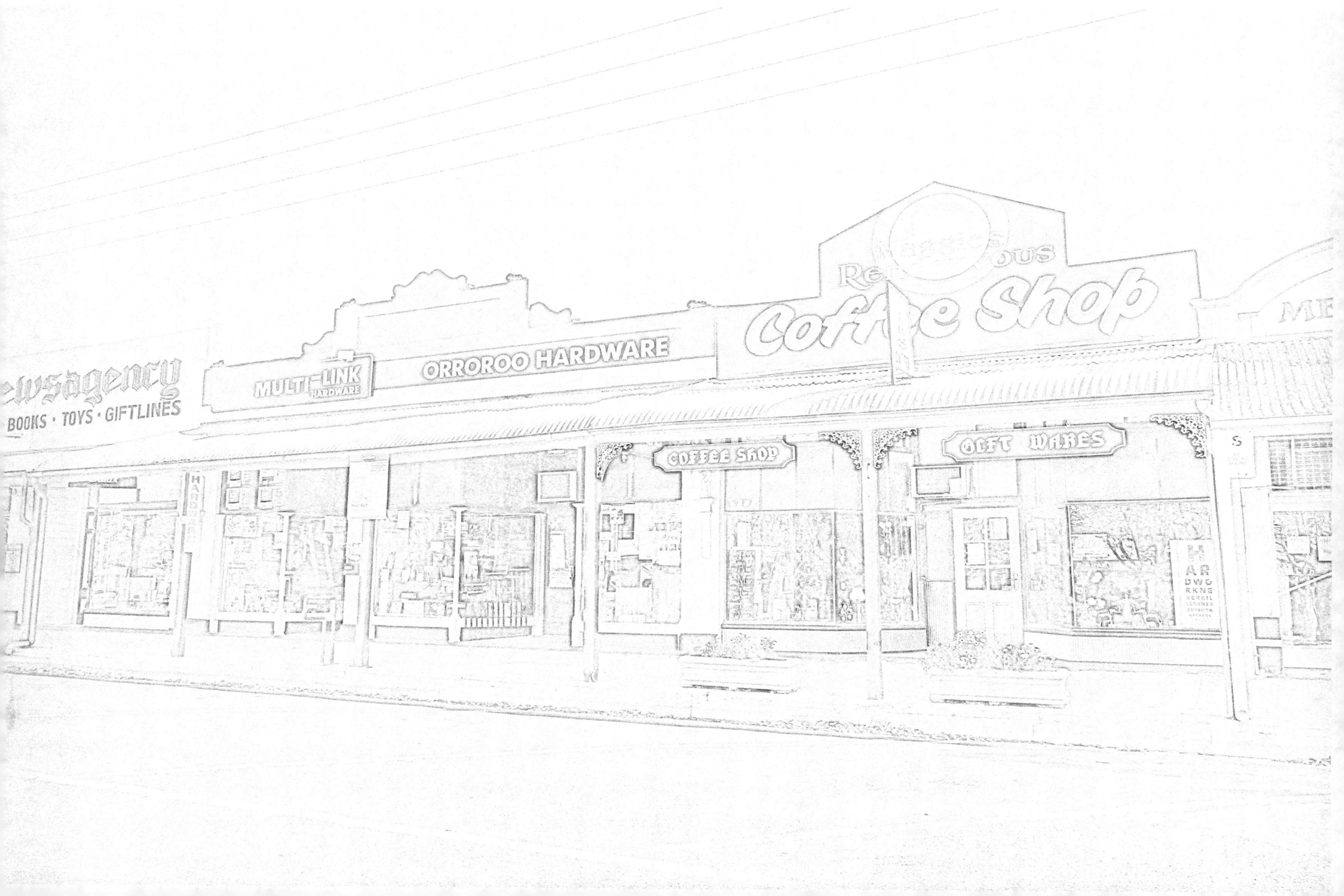
BOOKS · TOYS · GIFTLINES
MULTI-LINK
HARDWARE
ORROROO HARDWARE
Coffee Shop
COFFEE SHOP
GIFT WARES

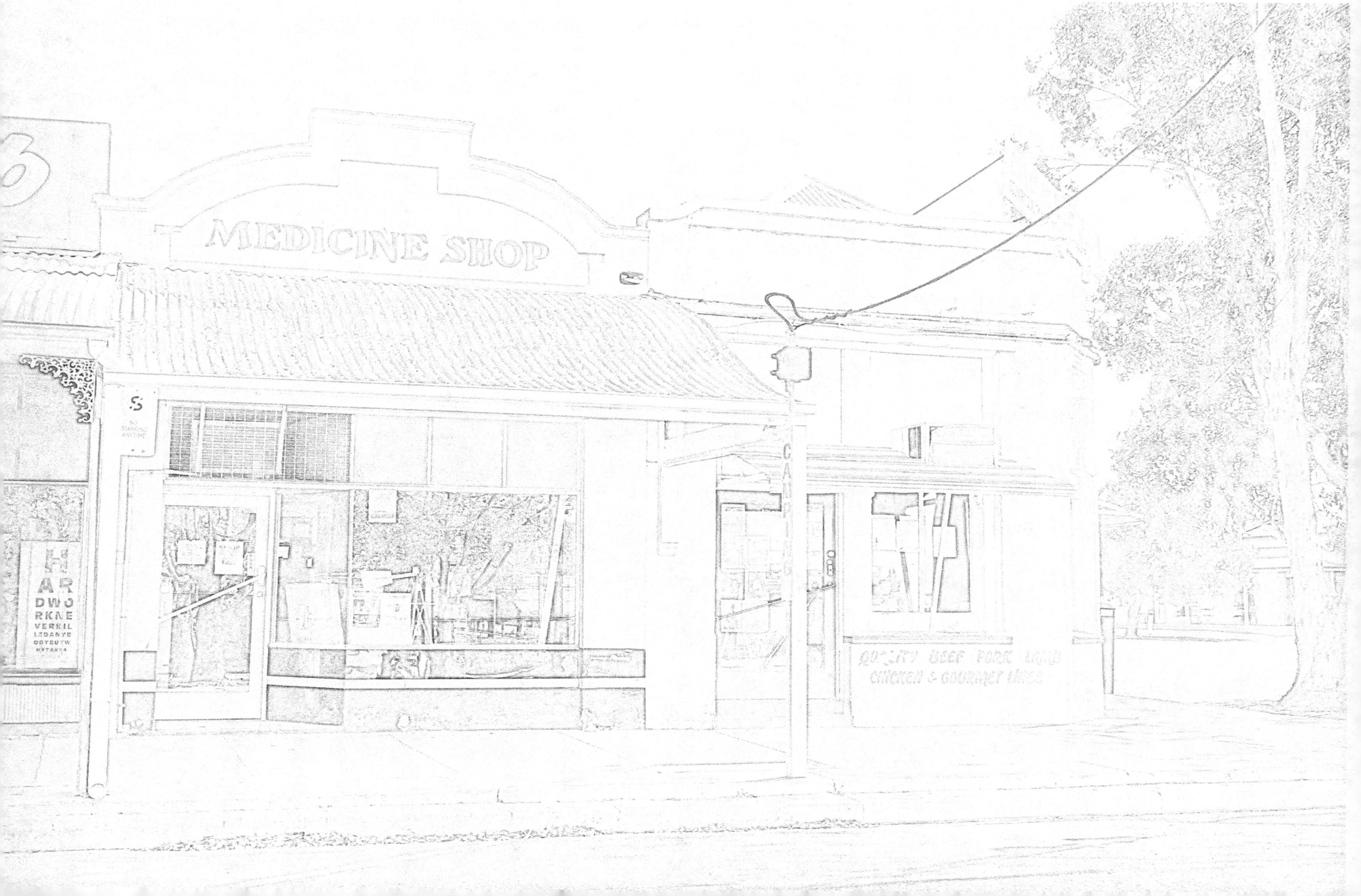
MEDICINE SHOP
NO STANDING ANYTIME
QUALITY BEEF PORK LAMB
CHICKEN & GOURMET LINES

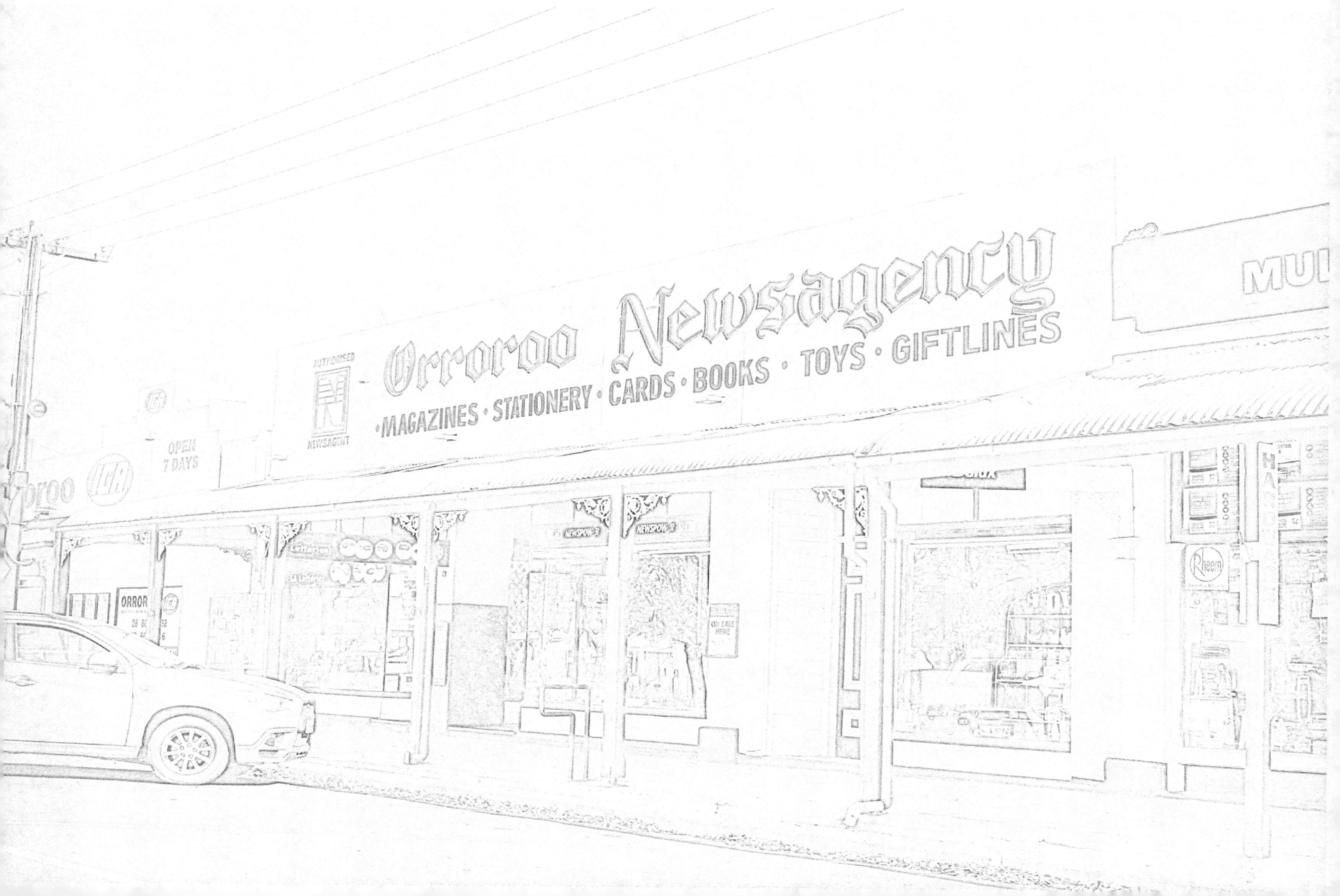
Orroroo Newsagency
·MAGAZINES · STATIONERY · CARDS · BOOKS · TOYS · GIFTLINES
AUTHORISED
NEWSAGENT
OPEN
7 DAYS
IGA
ON SALE
HERE
Rheem

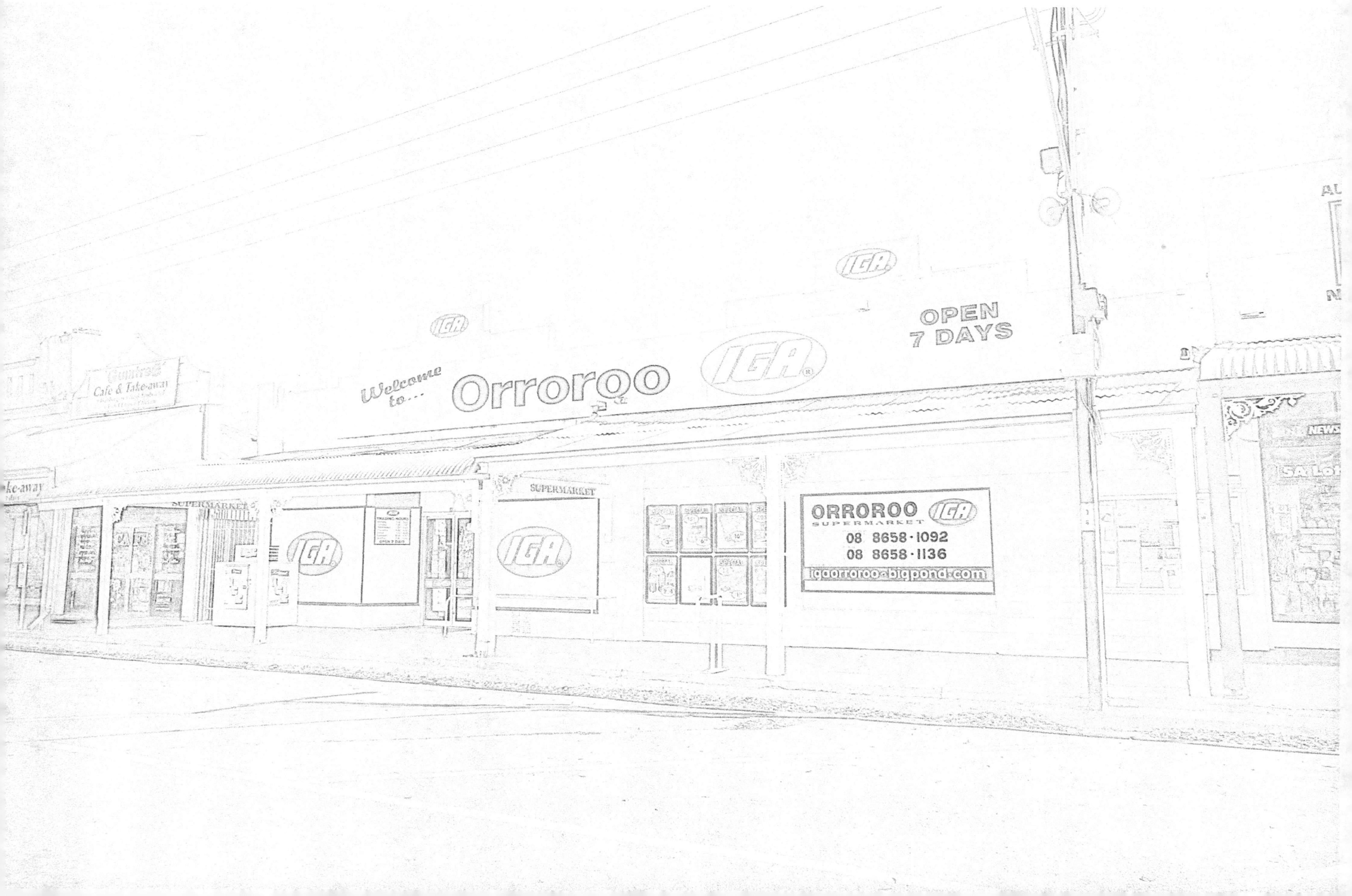
Welcome to...
Orroroo
IGA
OPEN
7 DAYS
Cafe & Take-away
SUPERMARKET
SUPERMARKET
ORROROO
SUPERMARKET
08 8658·1092
08 8658·1136
igaorroroo@bigpond.com
NEWS

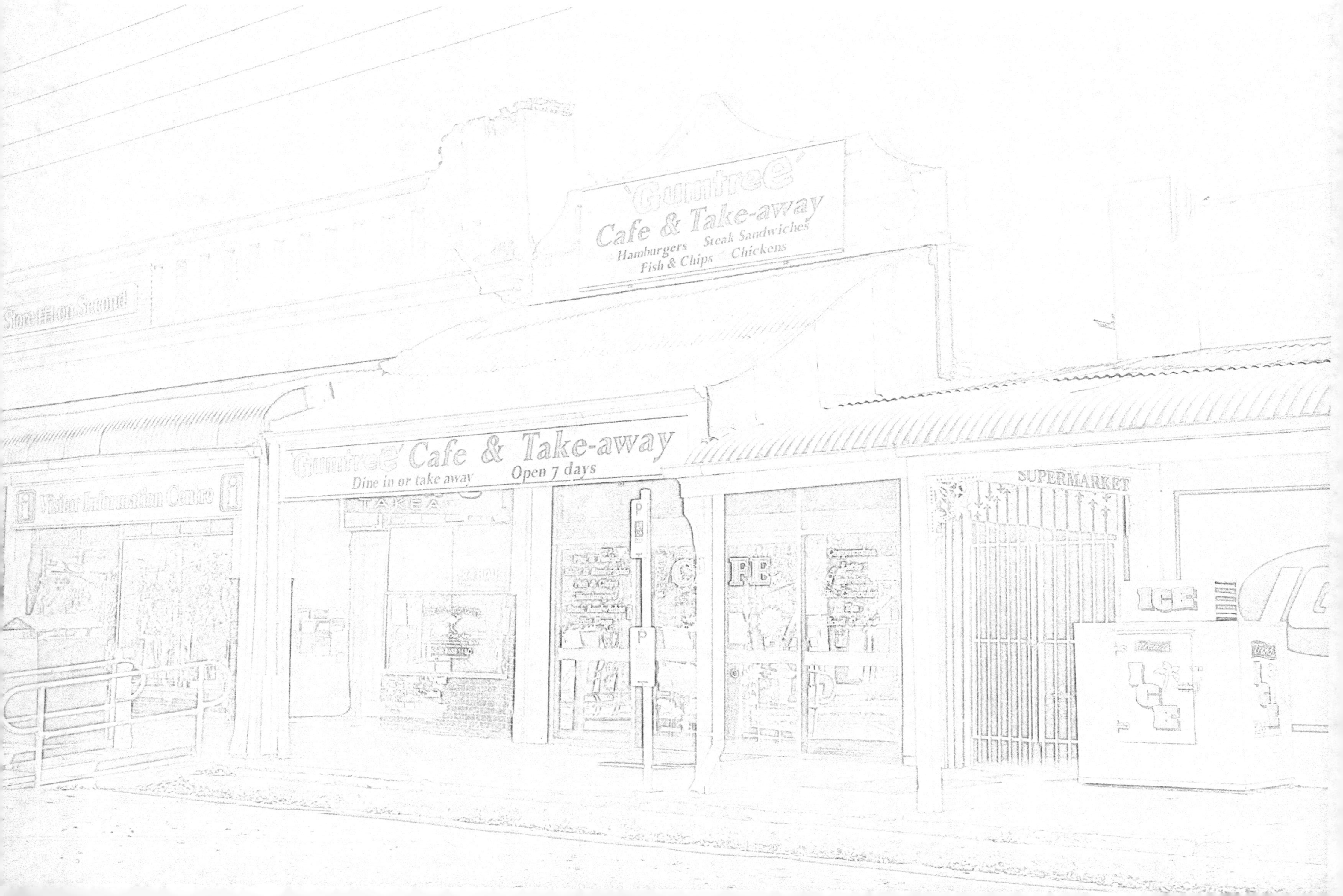
'Gumtree'
Cafe & Take-away
Hamburgers Steak Sandwiches
Fish & Chips Chickens
Store on Second
Visitor Information Centre
'Gumtree' Cafe & Take-away
Dine in or take away
Open 7 days
SUPERMARKET
ICE

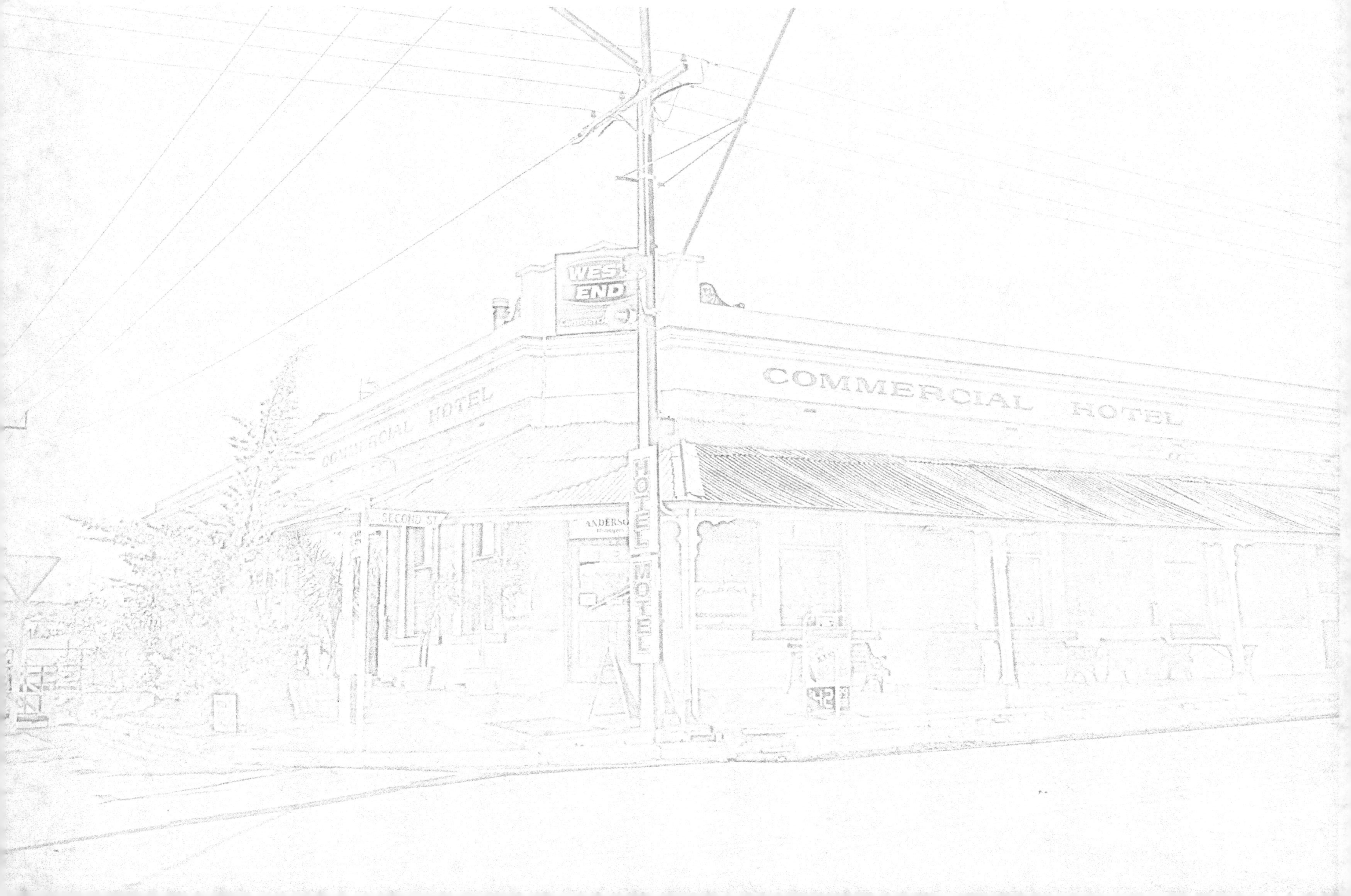
WEST
END
COMMERCIAL HOTEL
COMMERCIAL HOTEL
HOTEL
MOTEL
SECOND ST
ANDERSO

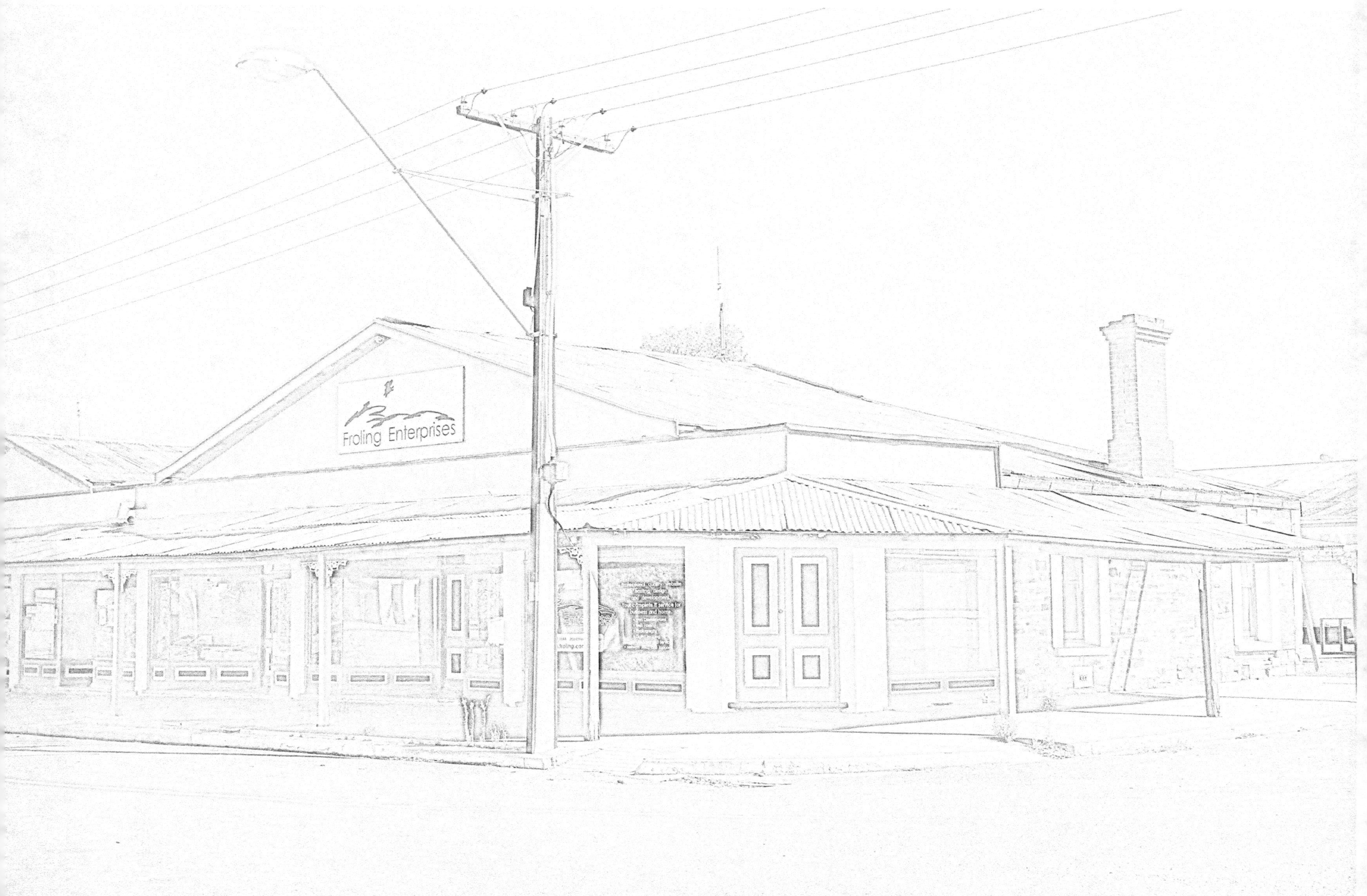
Froling Enterprises

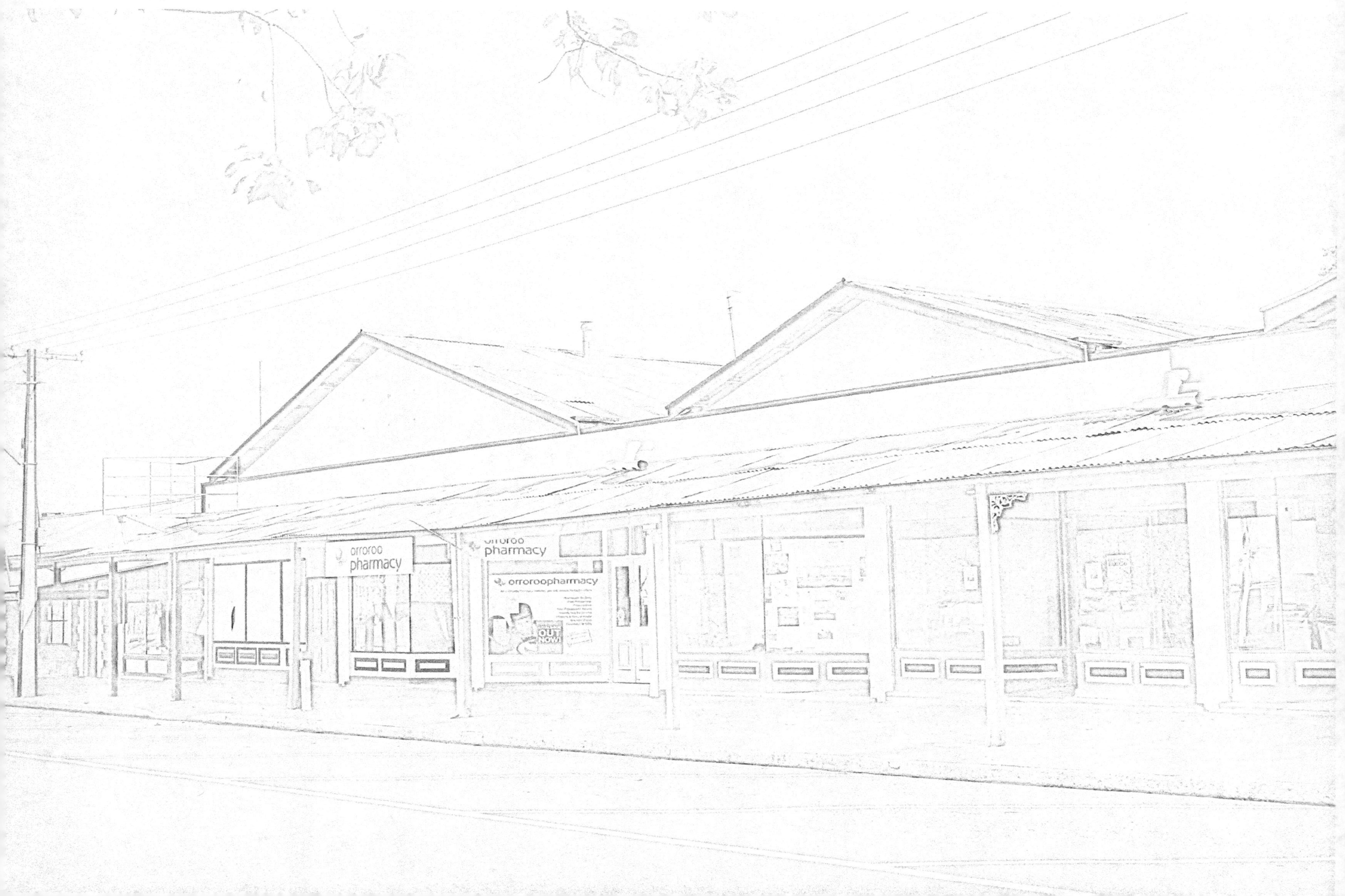
orroroo pharmacy
orroroo pharmacy
orroroopharmacy
OUT NOW!

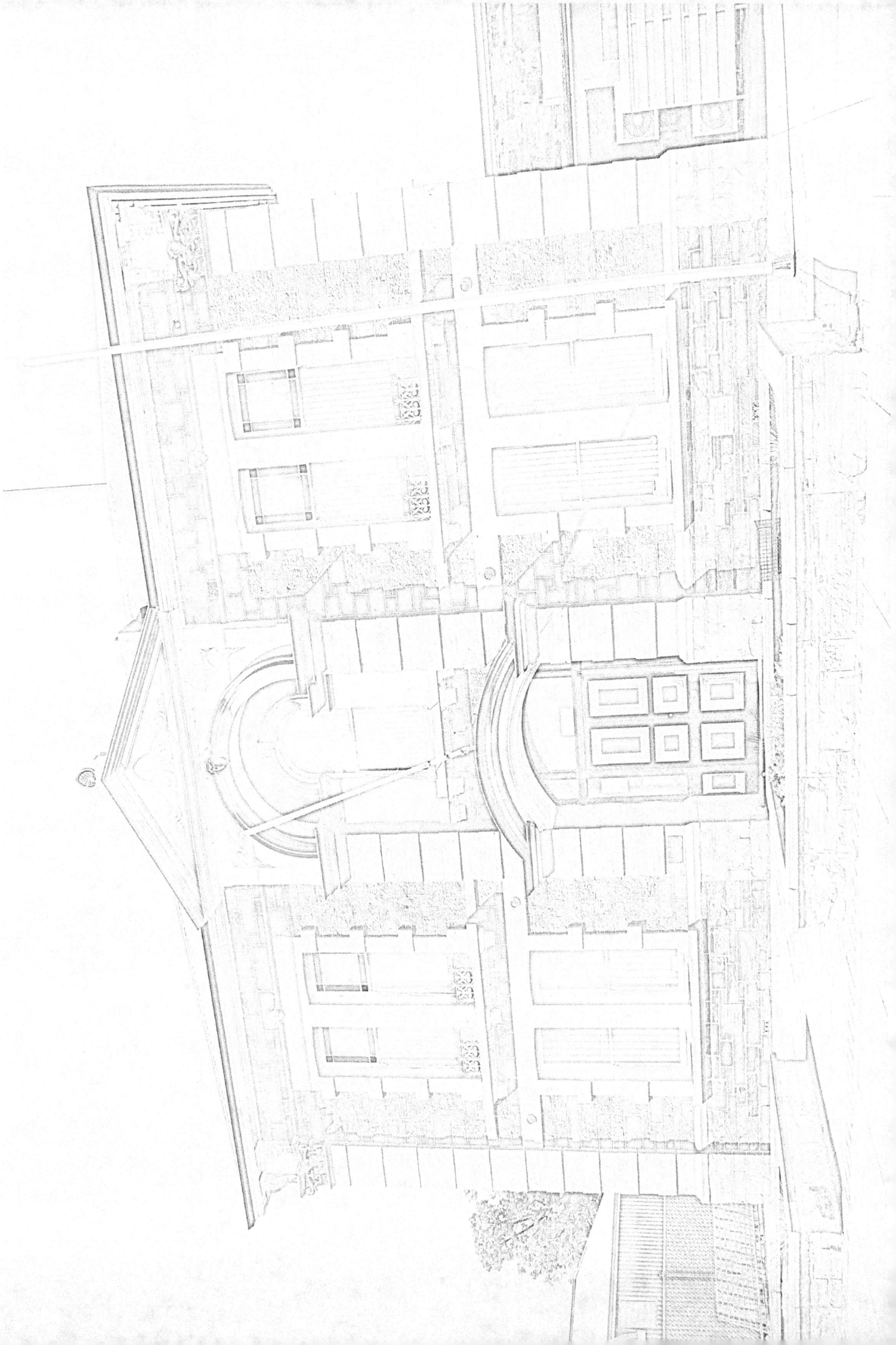

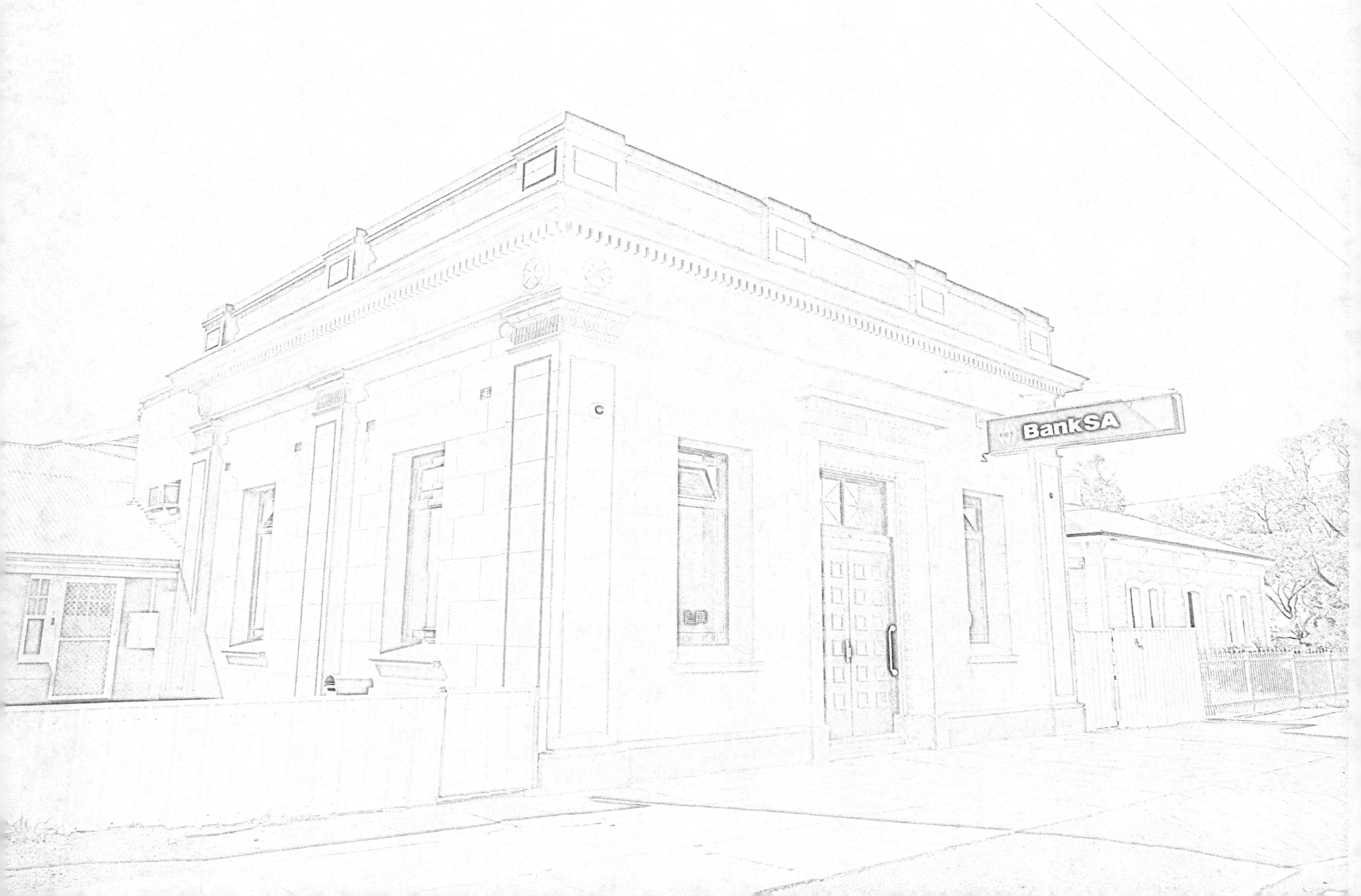
BankSA

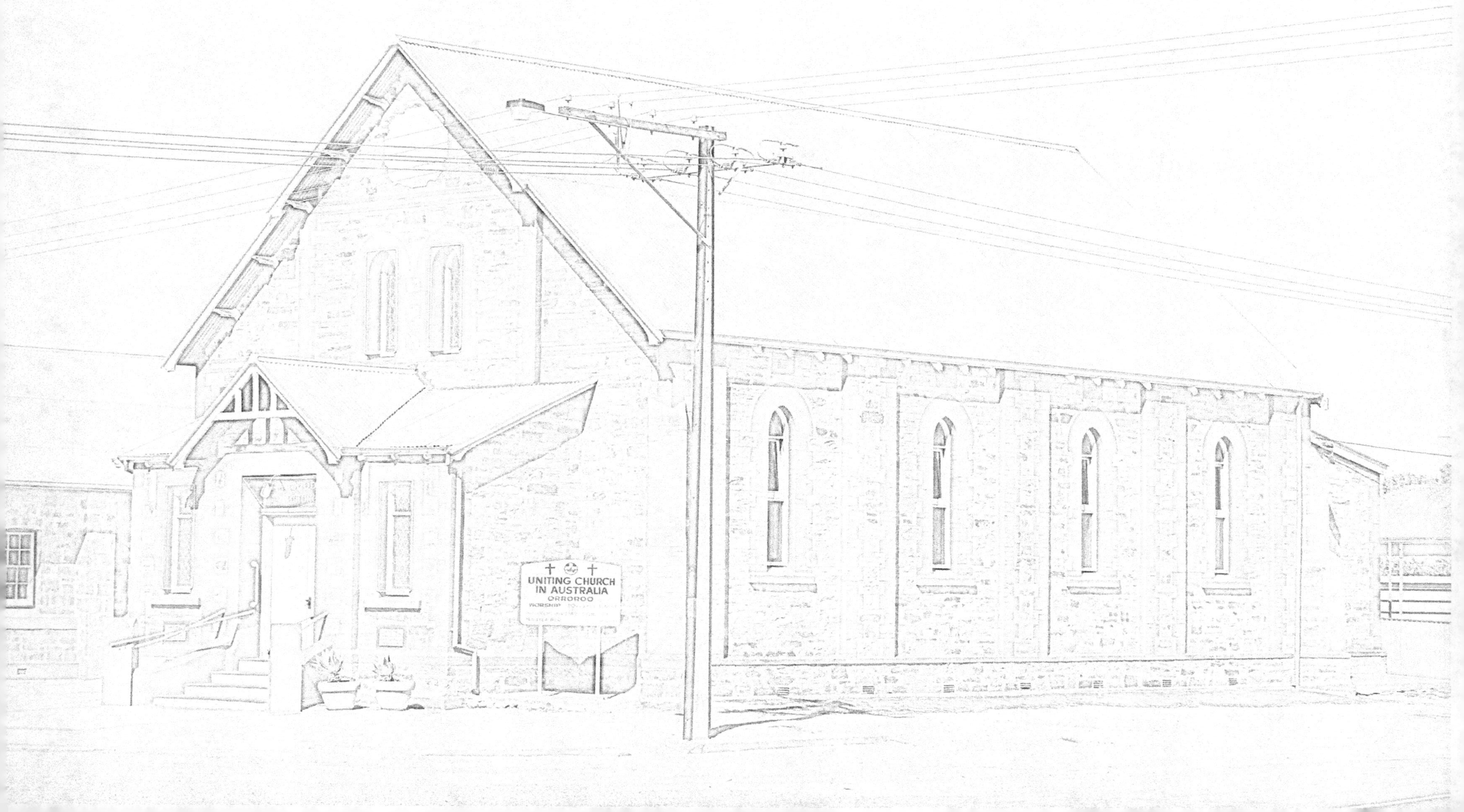
UNITING CHURCH
IN AUSTRALIA
ORROROO
WORSHIP

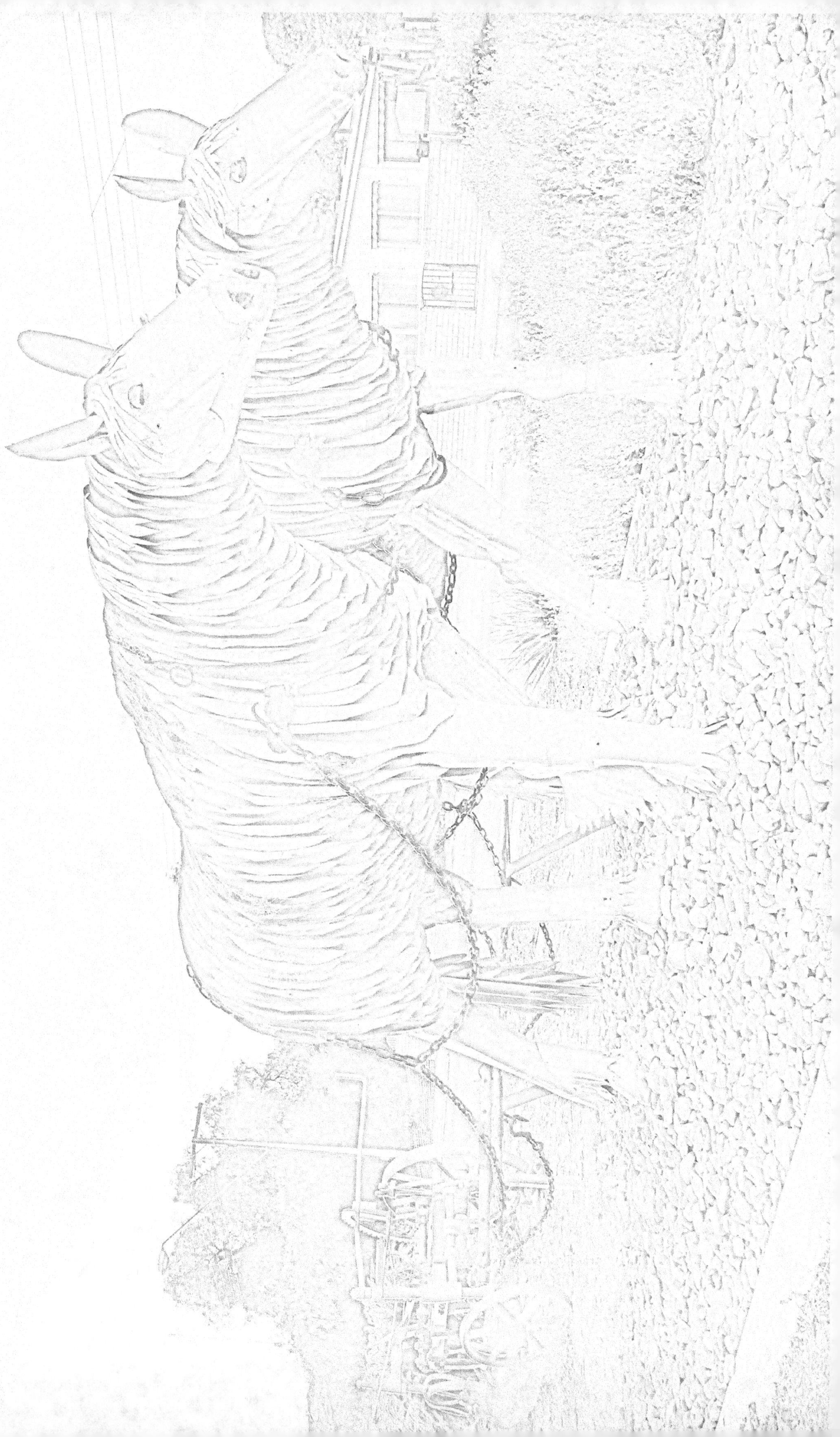

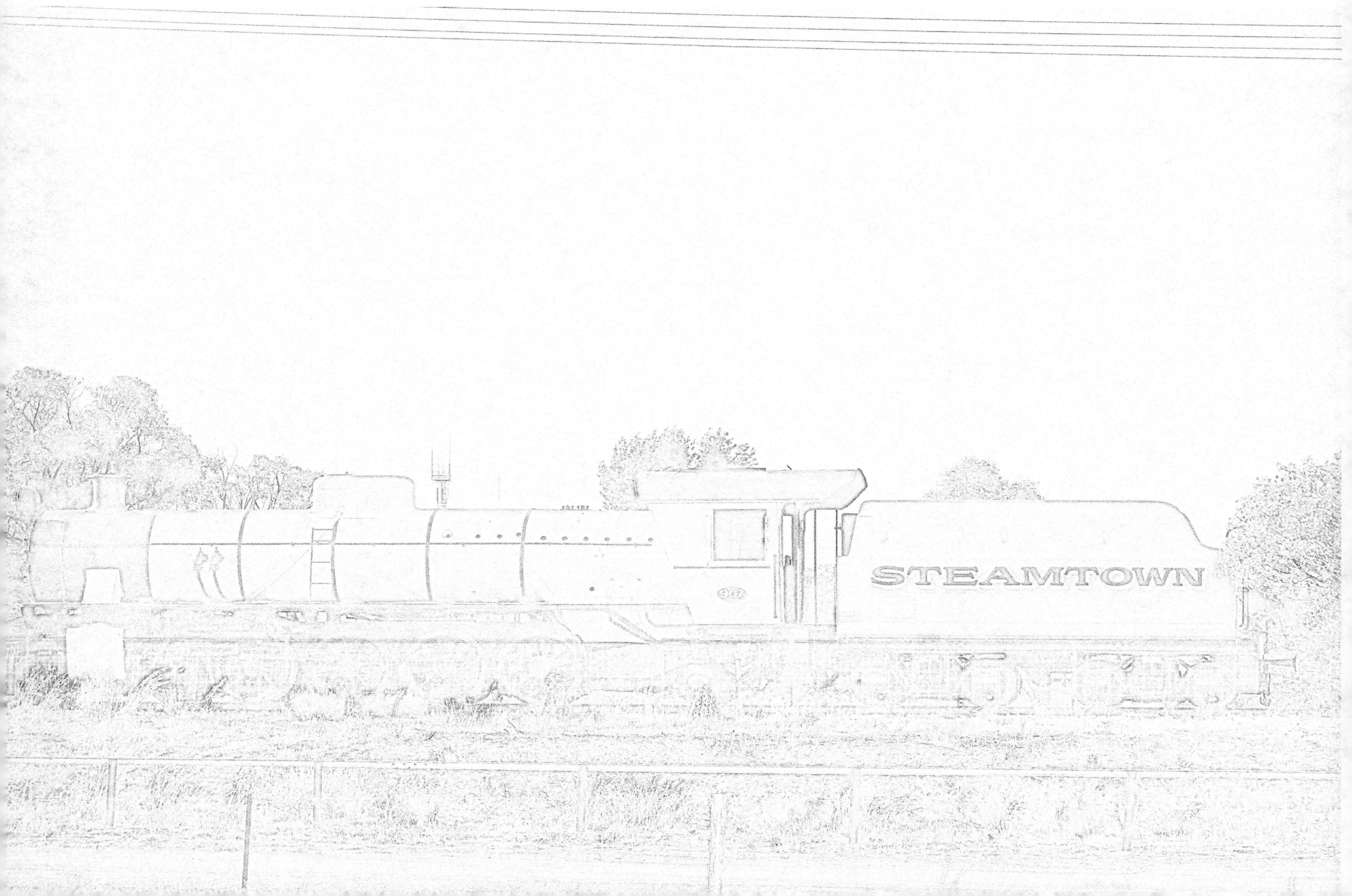
STEAMTOWN
907

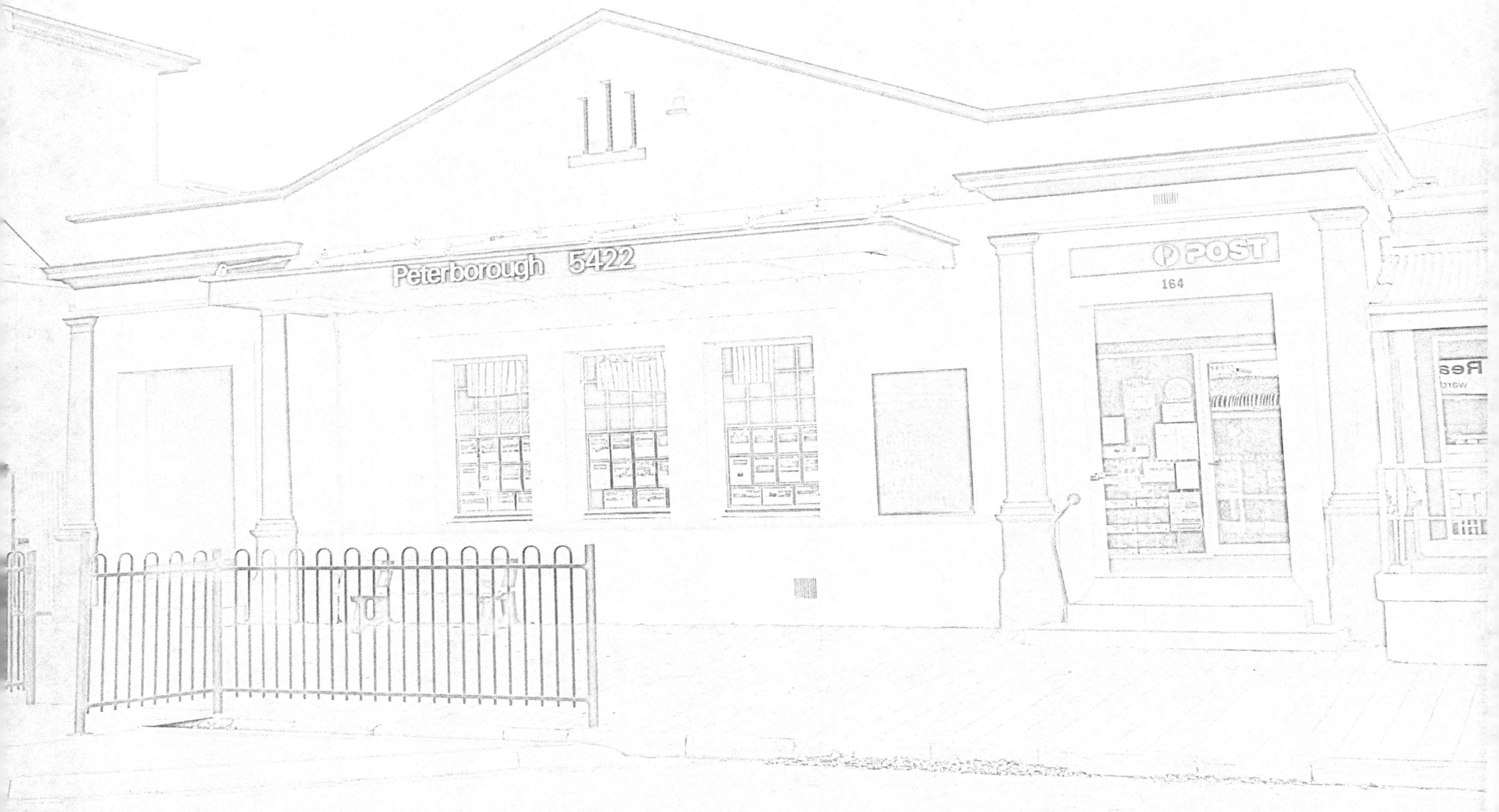
Peterborough 5422
POST
164

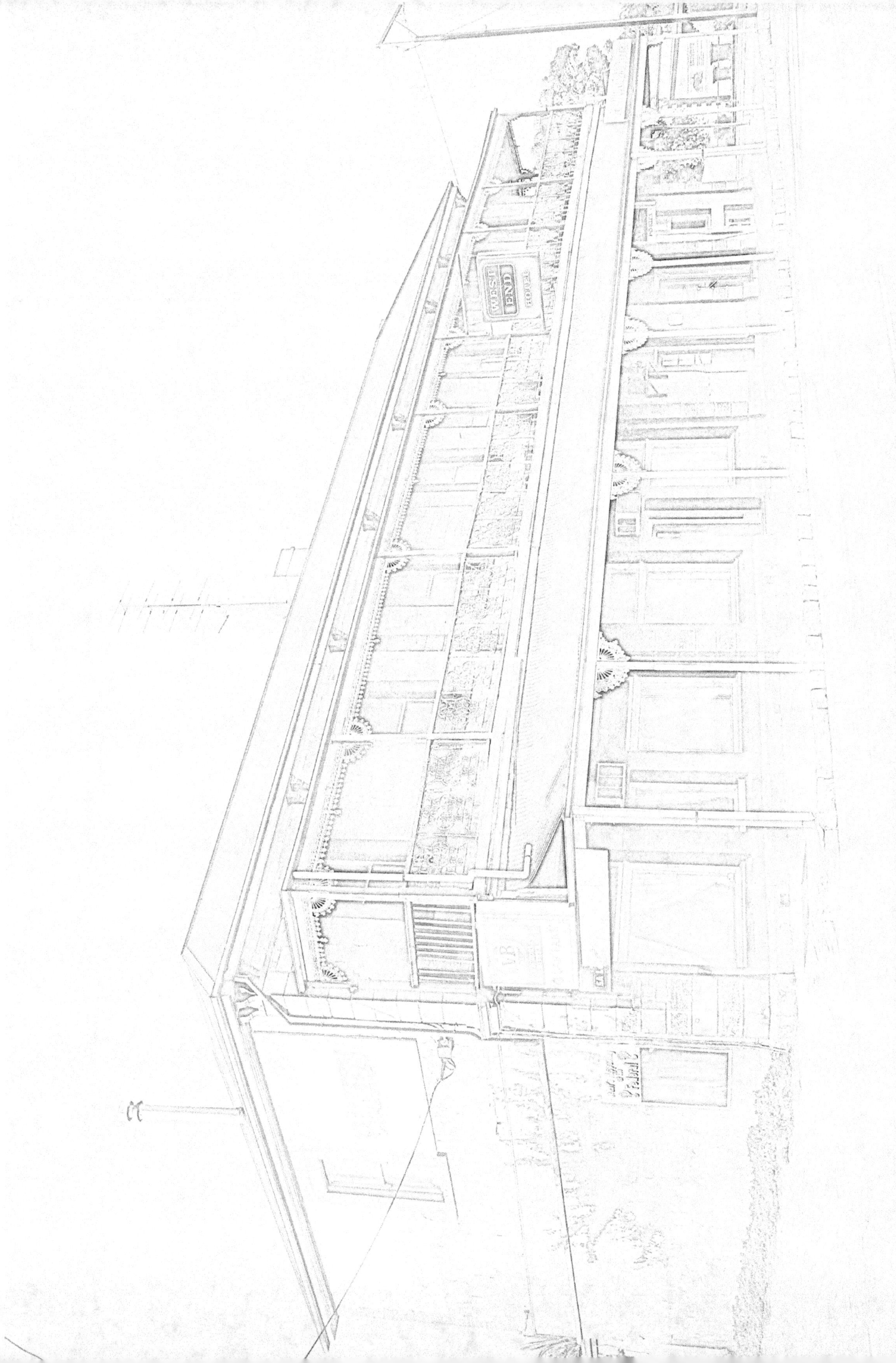
WEST
END
HOTEL
VB

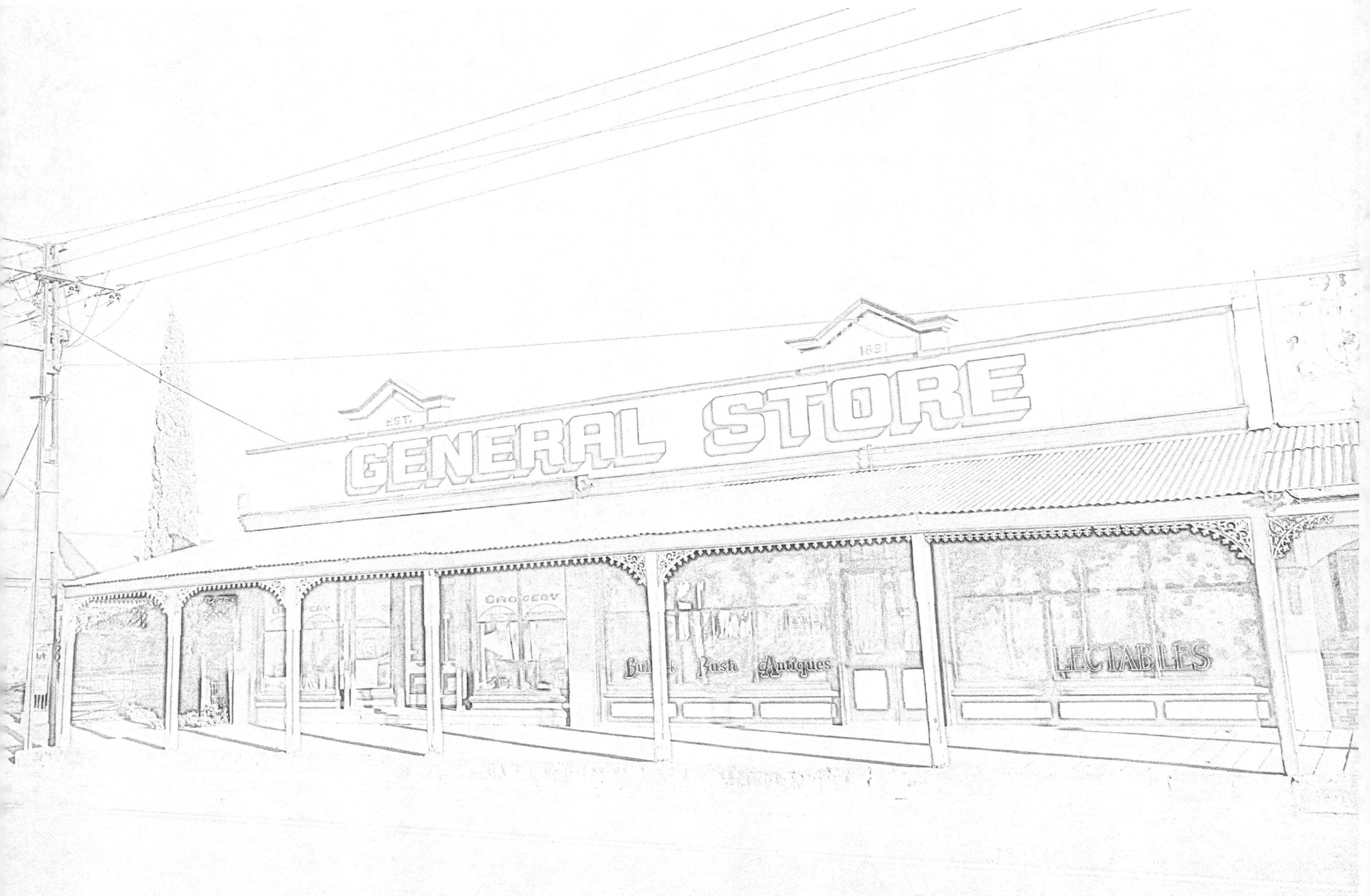
EST.
1891
GENERAL STORE
GROCERY
Bush Antiques
LECTABLES

VB VICTORIA BITTER
FEDERAL HOTEL
FED RAL HOTEL
VB VICTORIA BITTER

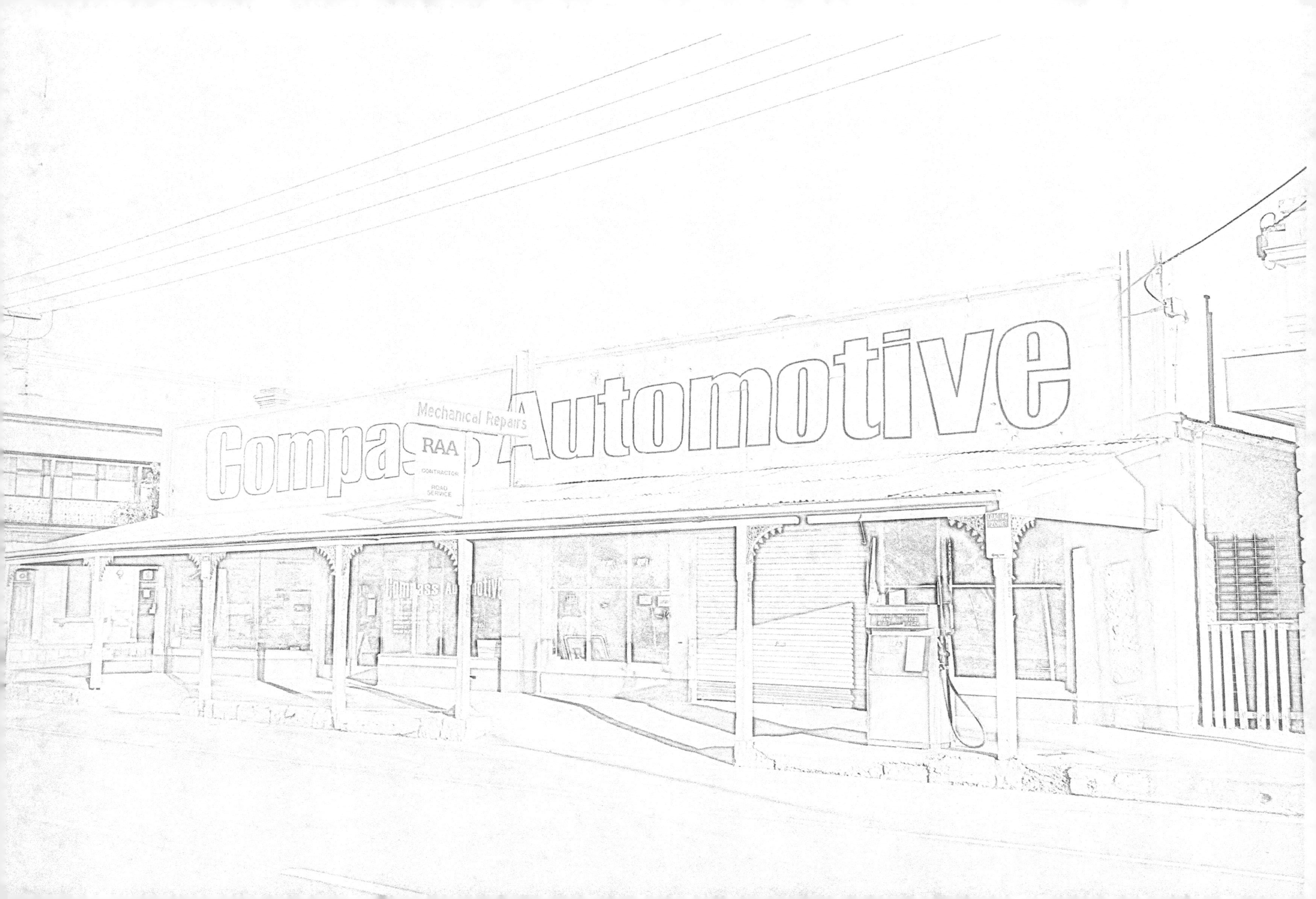
Mechanical Repairs
Compass Automotive
RAA
CONTRACTOR
ROAD SERVICE

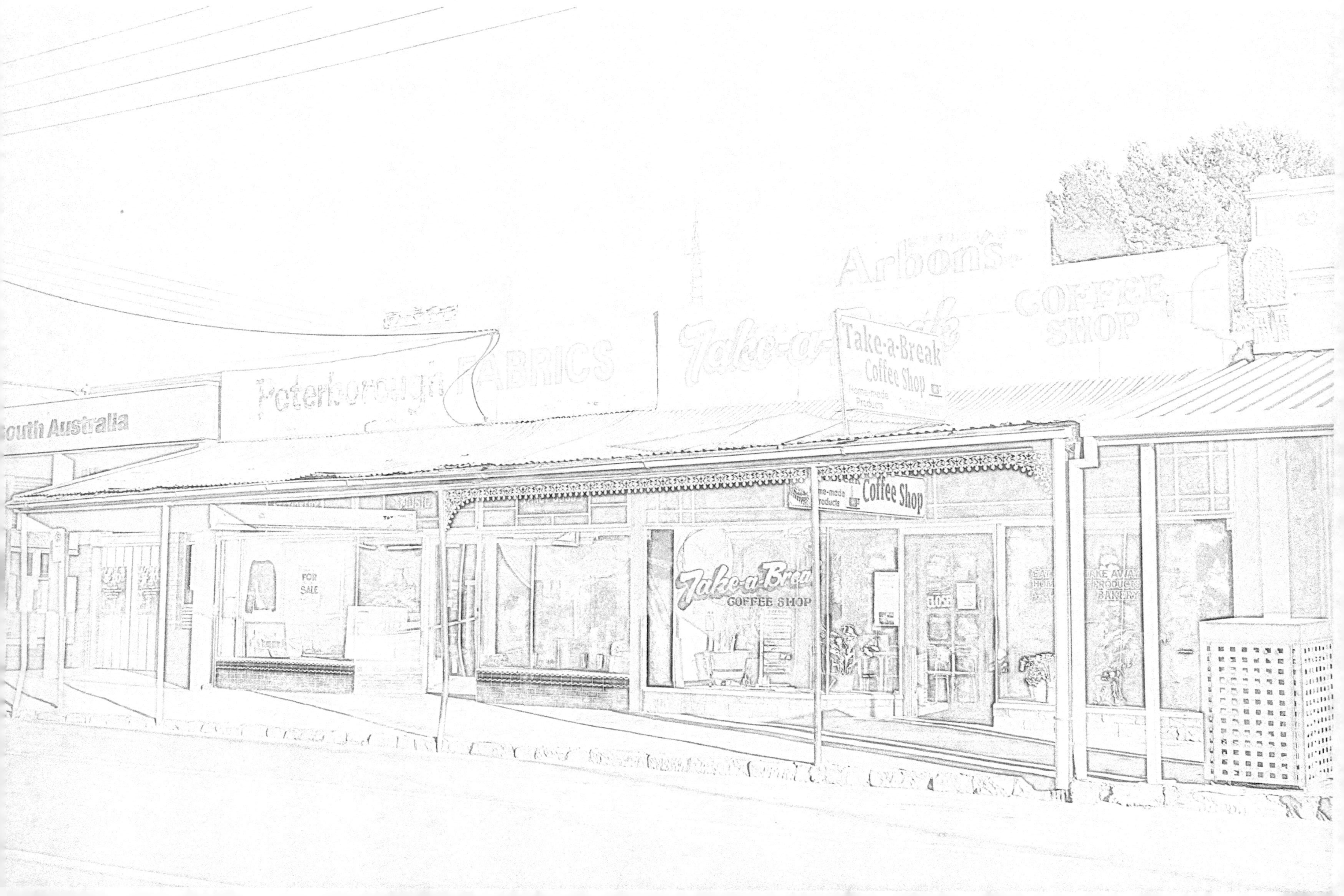

Arbon's
COFFEE SHOP
Take-a-Break
Coffee Shop
Home-made Products
Peterborough FABRICS
South Australia
Coffee Shop
Take-a-Break
COFFEE SHOP
FOR SALE
BAKERY

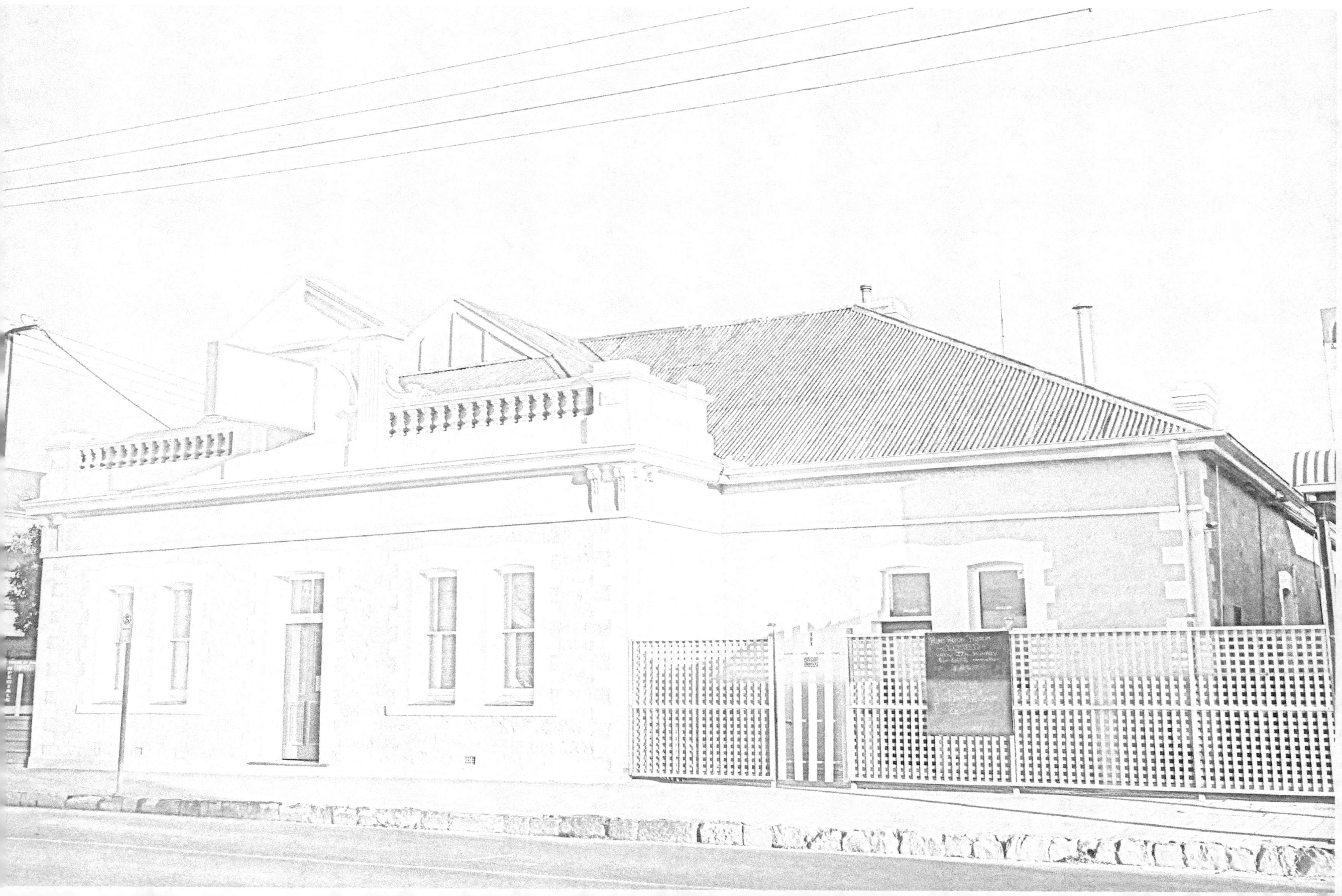

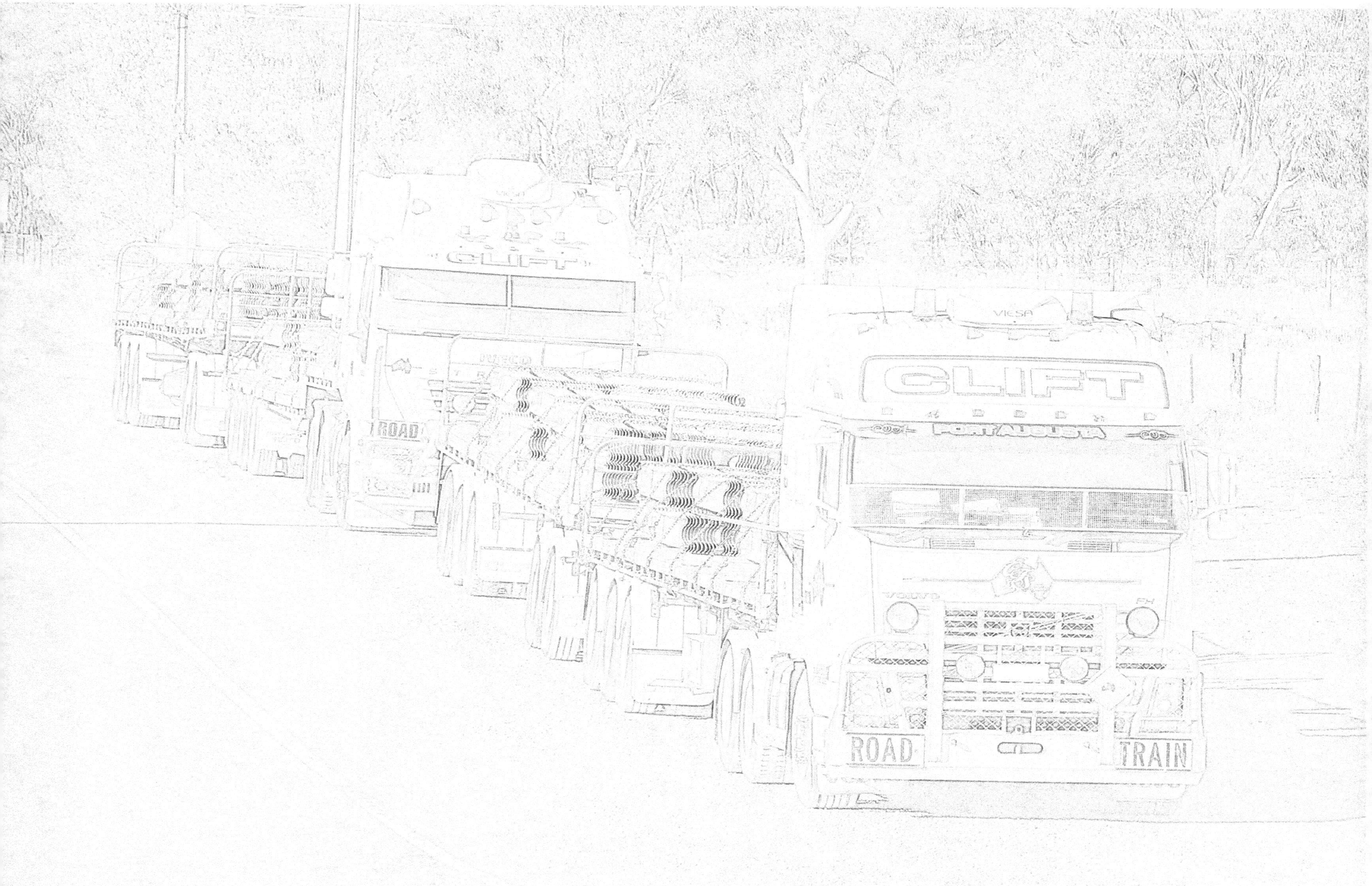

CLIFT
PORT AUGUSTA
ROAD TRAIN
CLIFT
ROAD

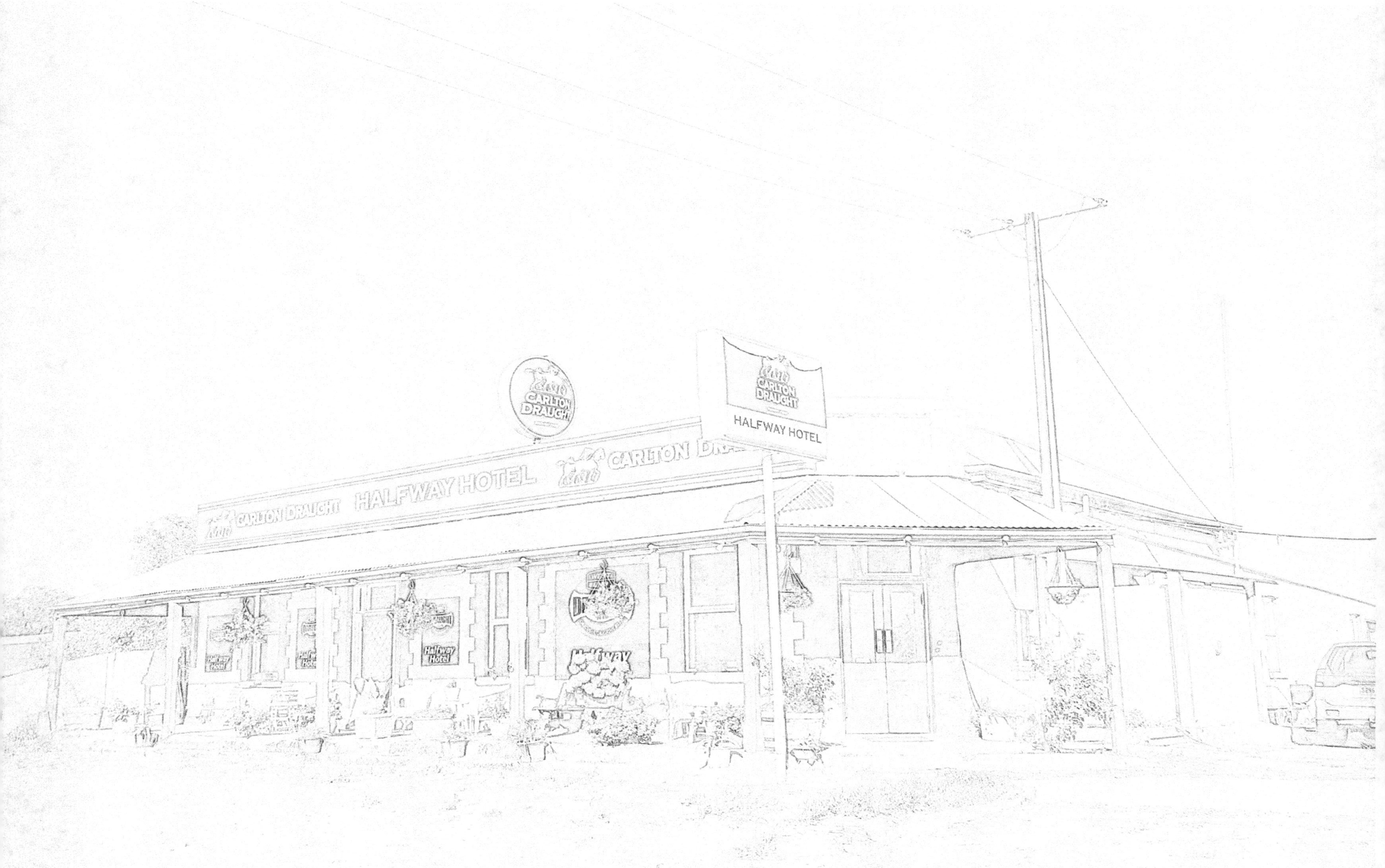
CARLTON DRAUGHT
HALFWAY HOTEL
CARLTON DRAUGHT
CARLTON DRAUGHT
HALFWAY HOTEL
CARLTON DR
Halfway Hotel
Halfway

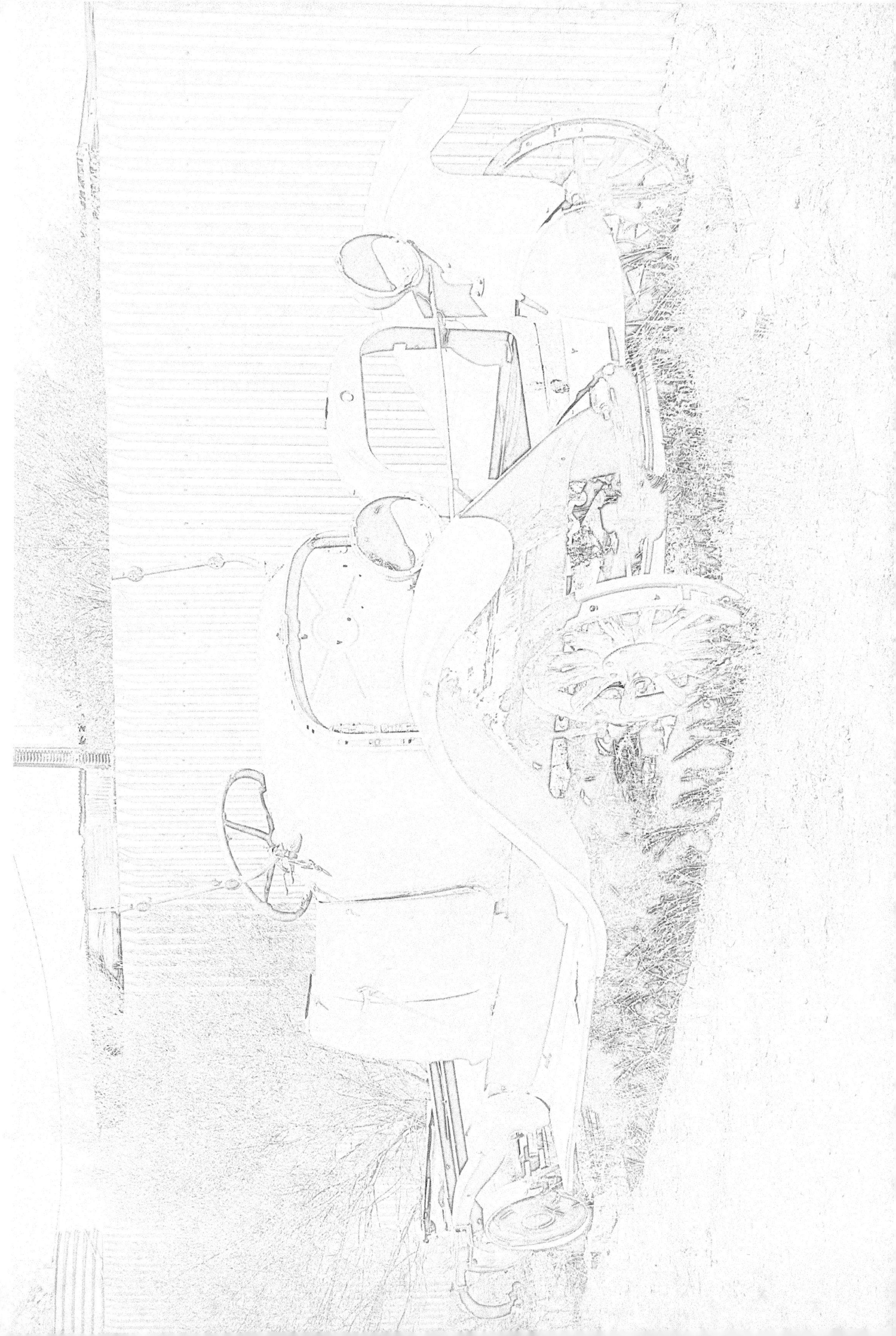

WELCOM

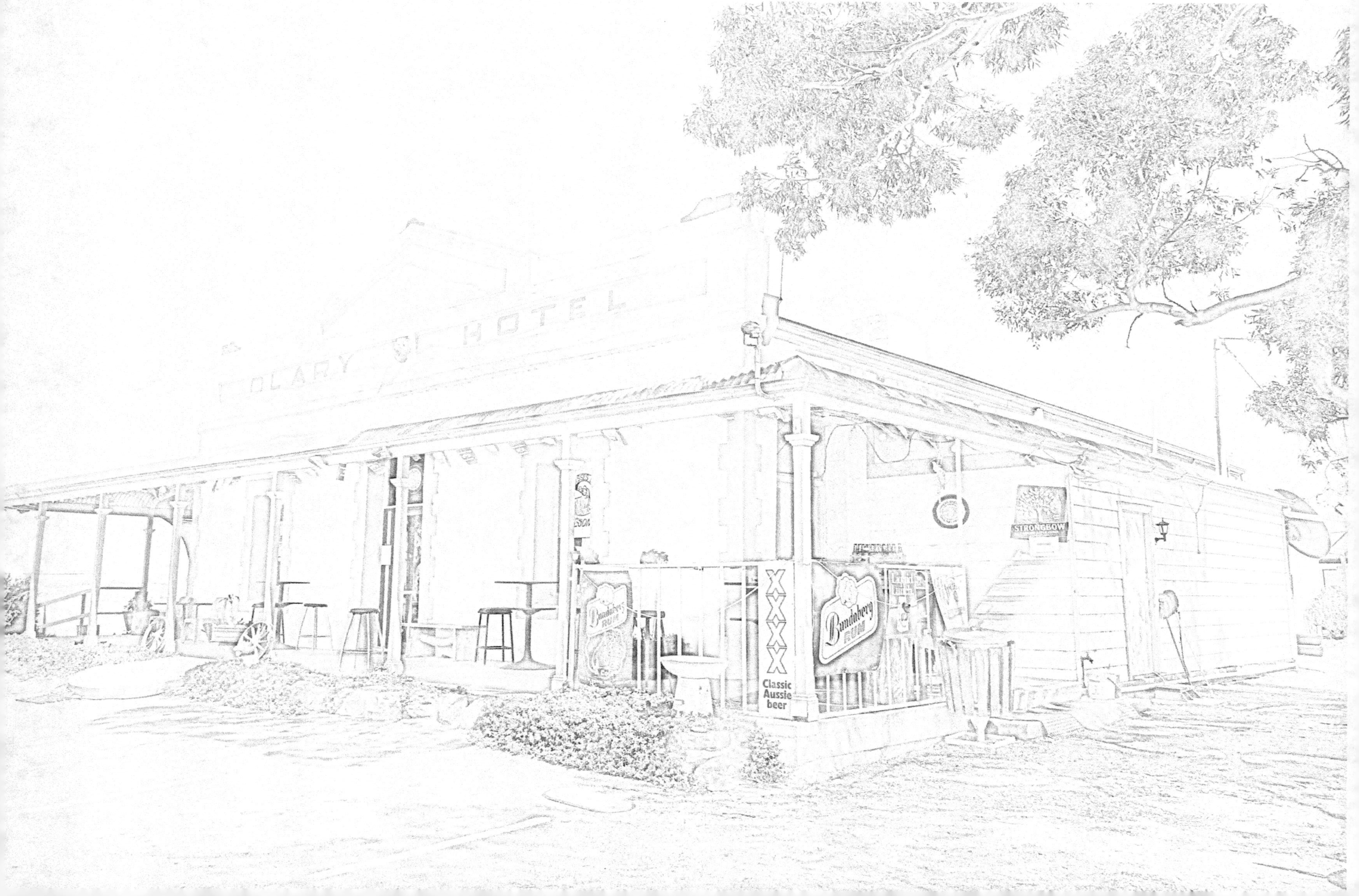
OLARY HOTEL
STRONGBOW
Bundaberg RUM
XXXX
Classic Aussie beer
Bundaberg RUM

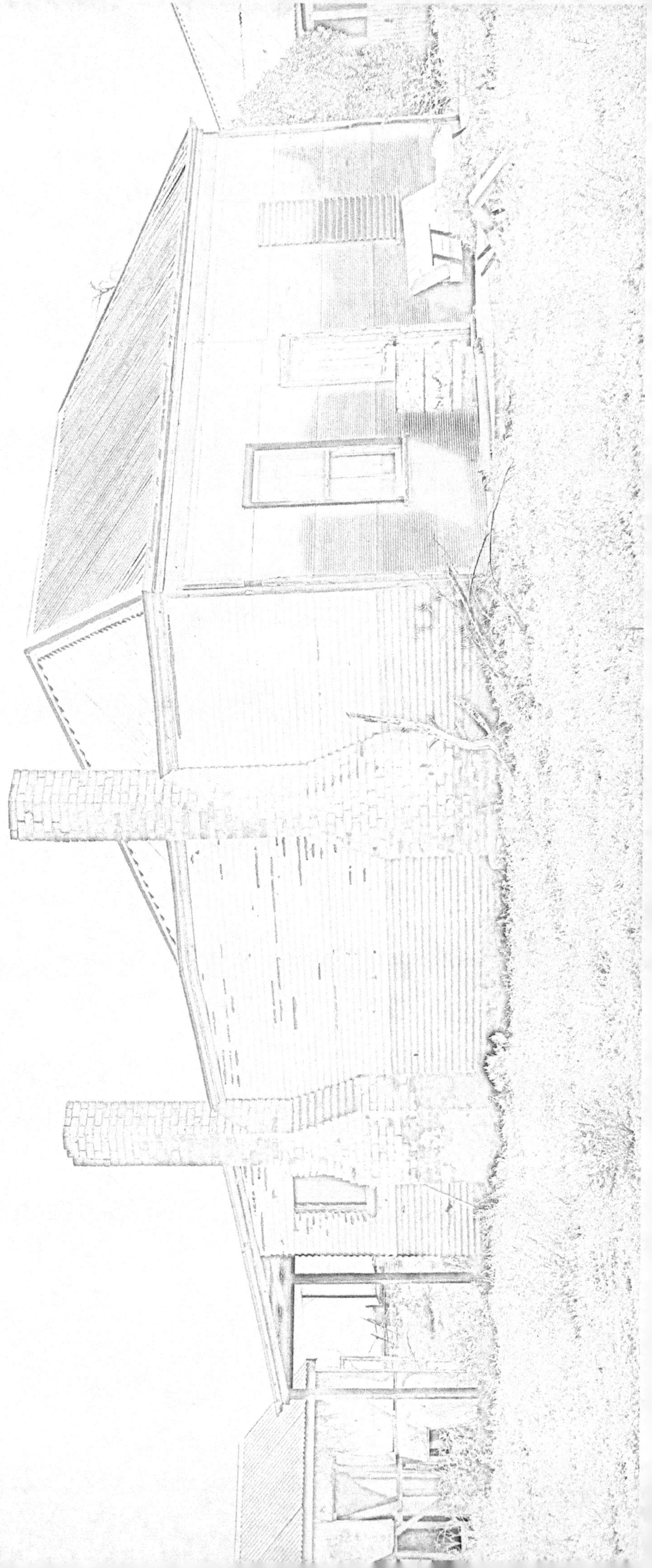

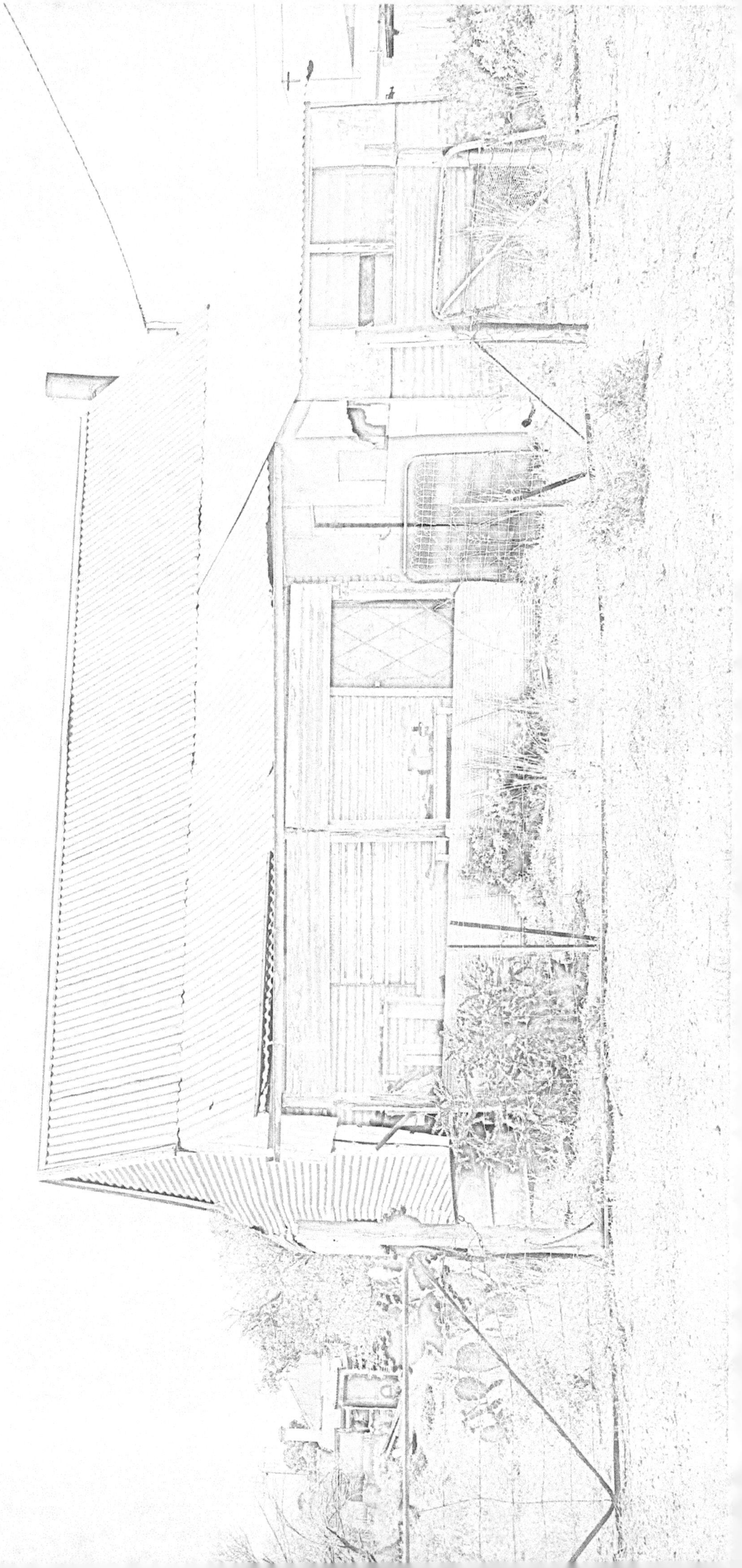

THE MAJ GALLERY
HER MAJESTY'S THEATRE
MAJESTYS
THE MAJ GALLERY
HER MAJESTY'S THEATRE AN ADELAIDE FESTIVAL CENTRE VENUE
THE MAJ GALLERY
THRILL
METROPOLITAN

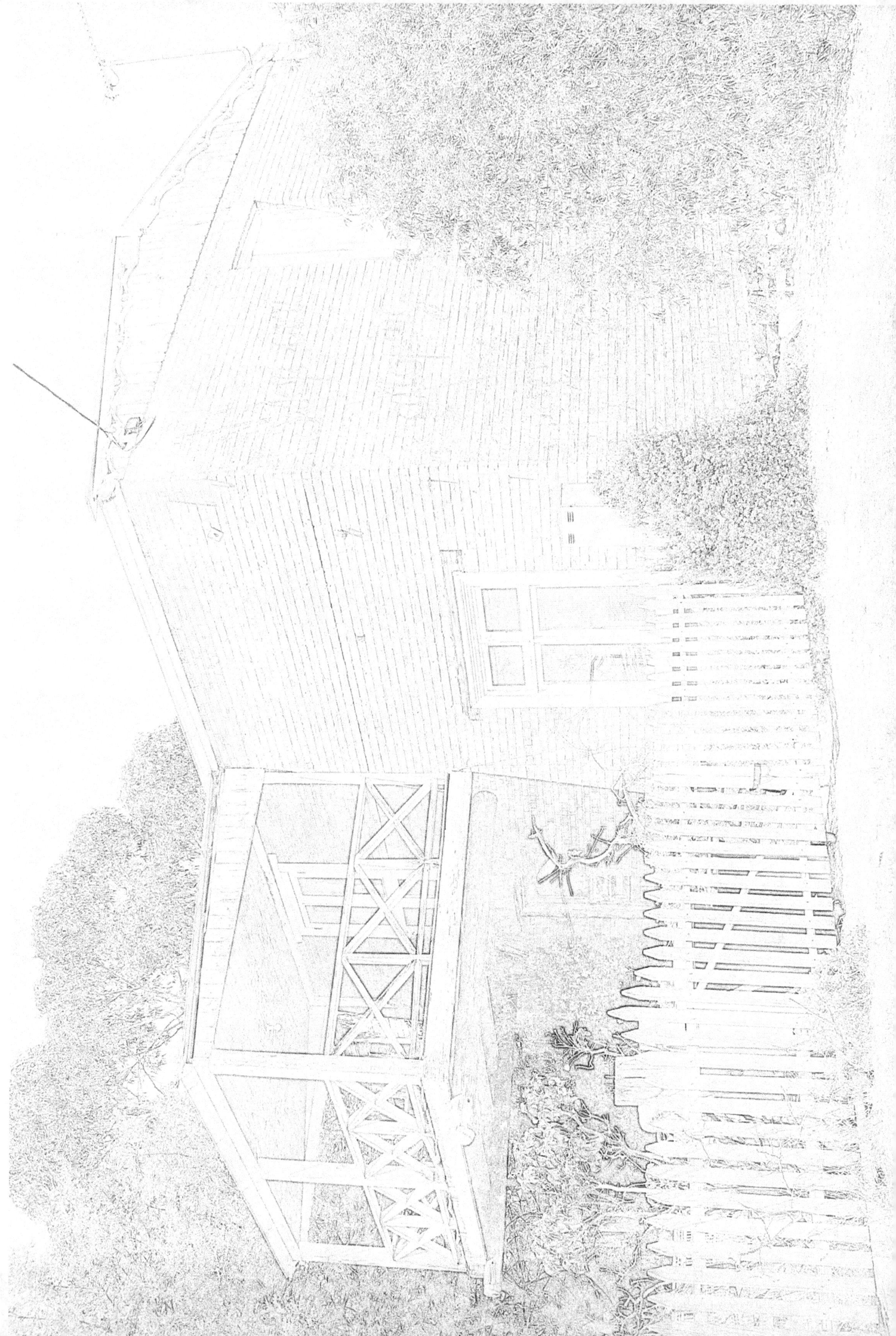

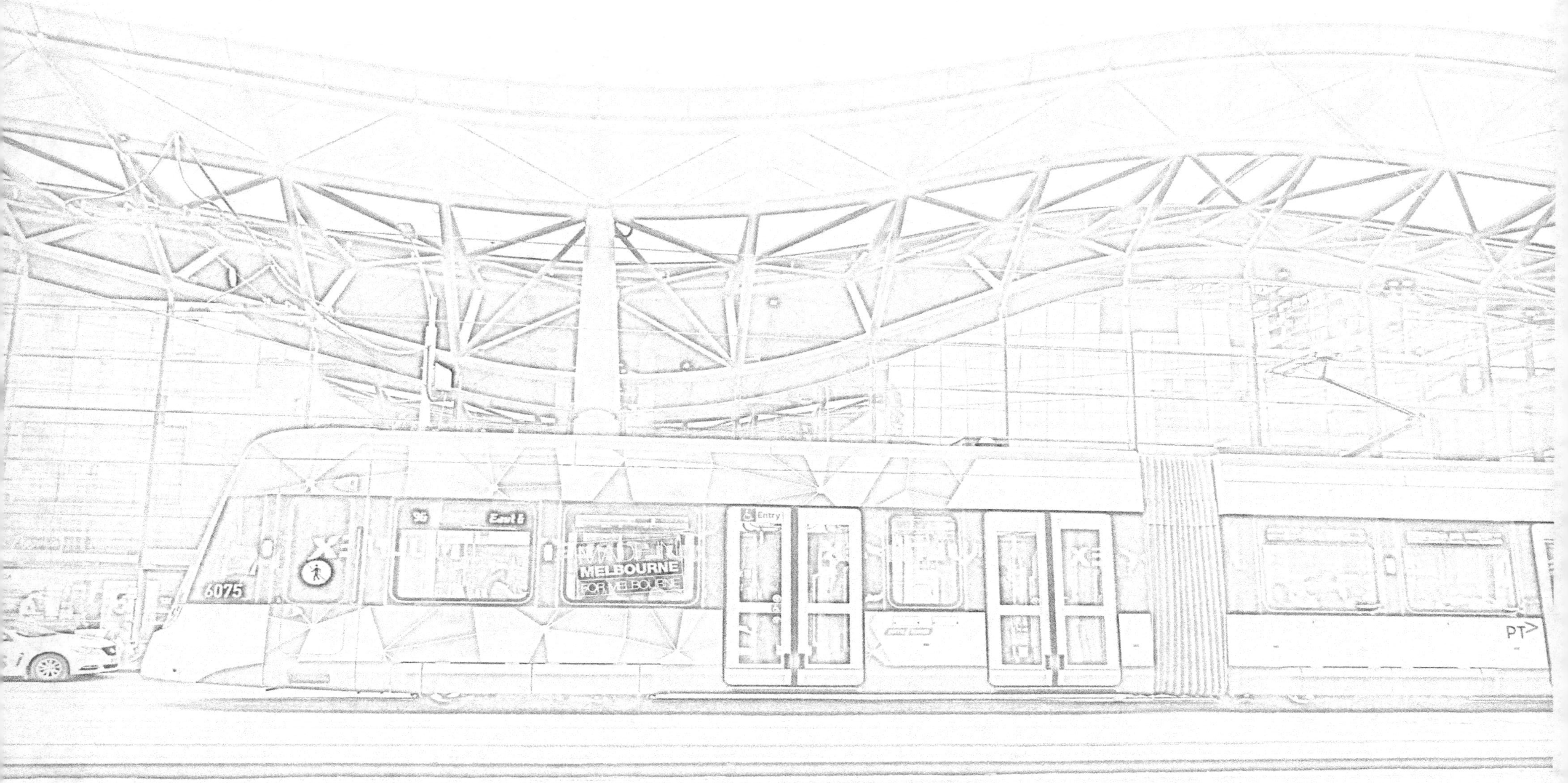
96
MELBOURNE
6075
Entry
PT>

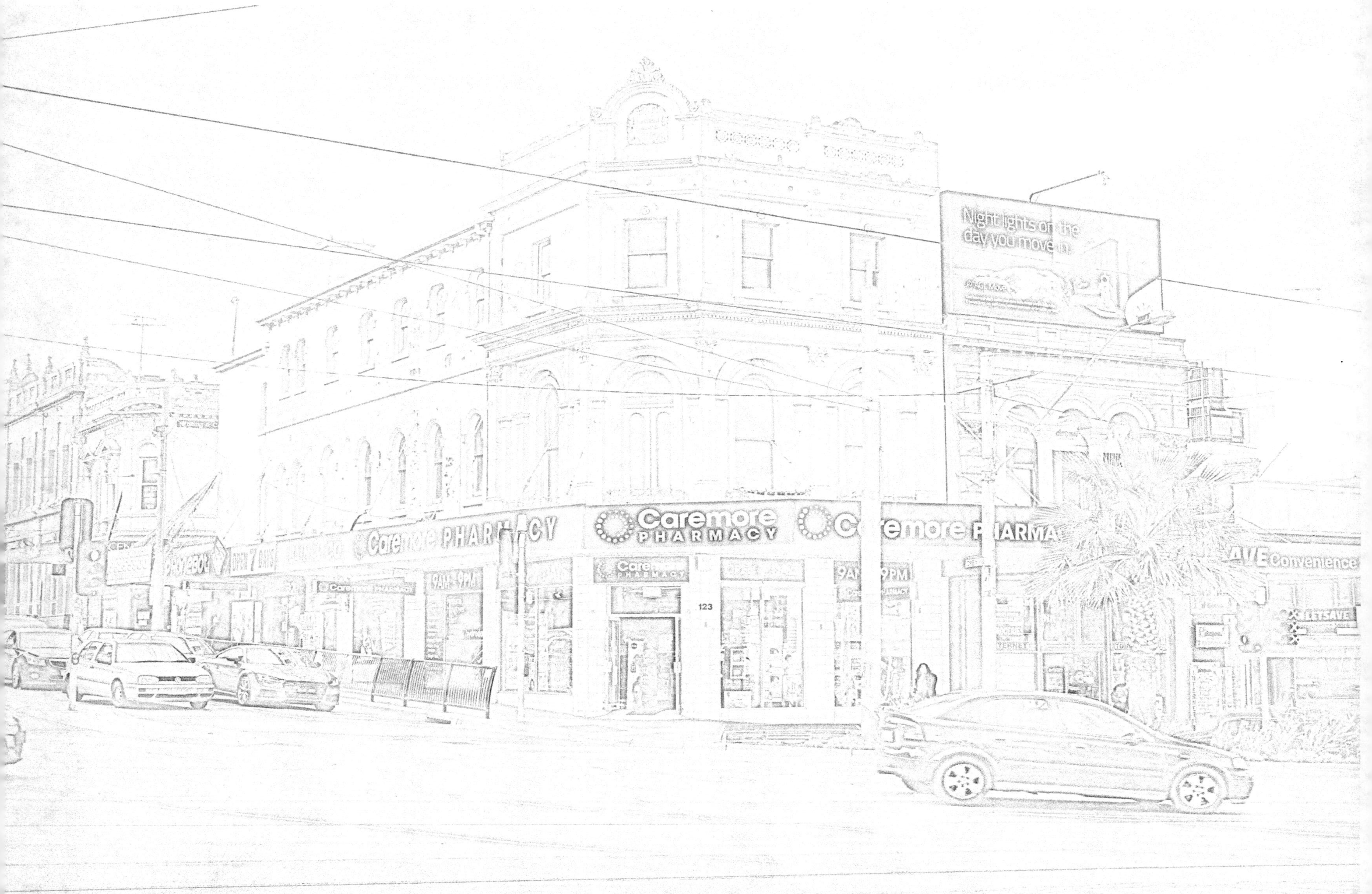
Night lights on the
day you move in.
Caremore
PHARMACY
Caremore PHARMA
Caremore PHAR ACY
OPEN 7 DAYS
9AM - 9PM
123
Convenience
LETSAVE

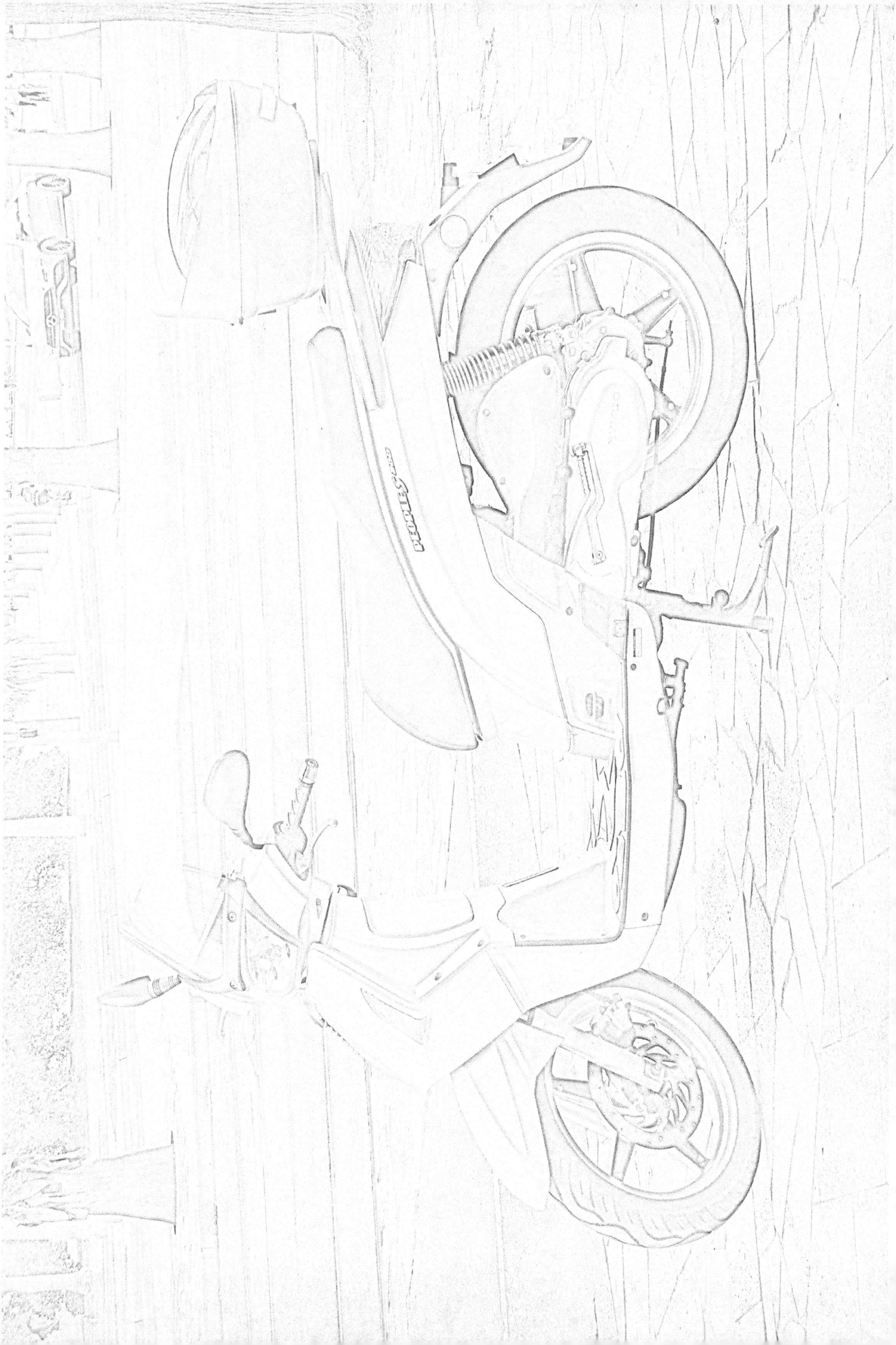

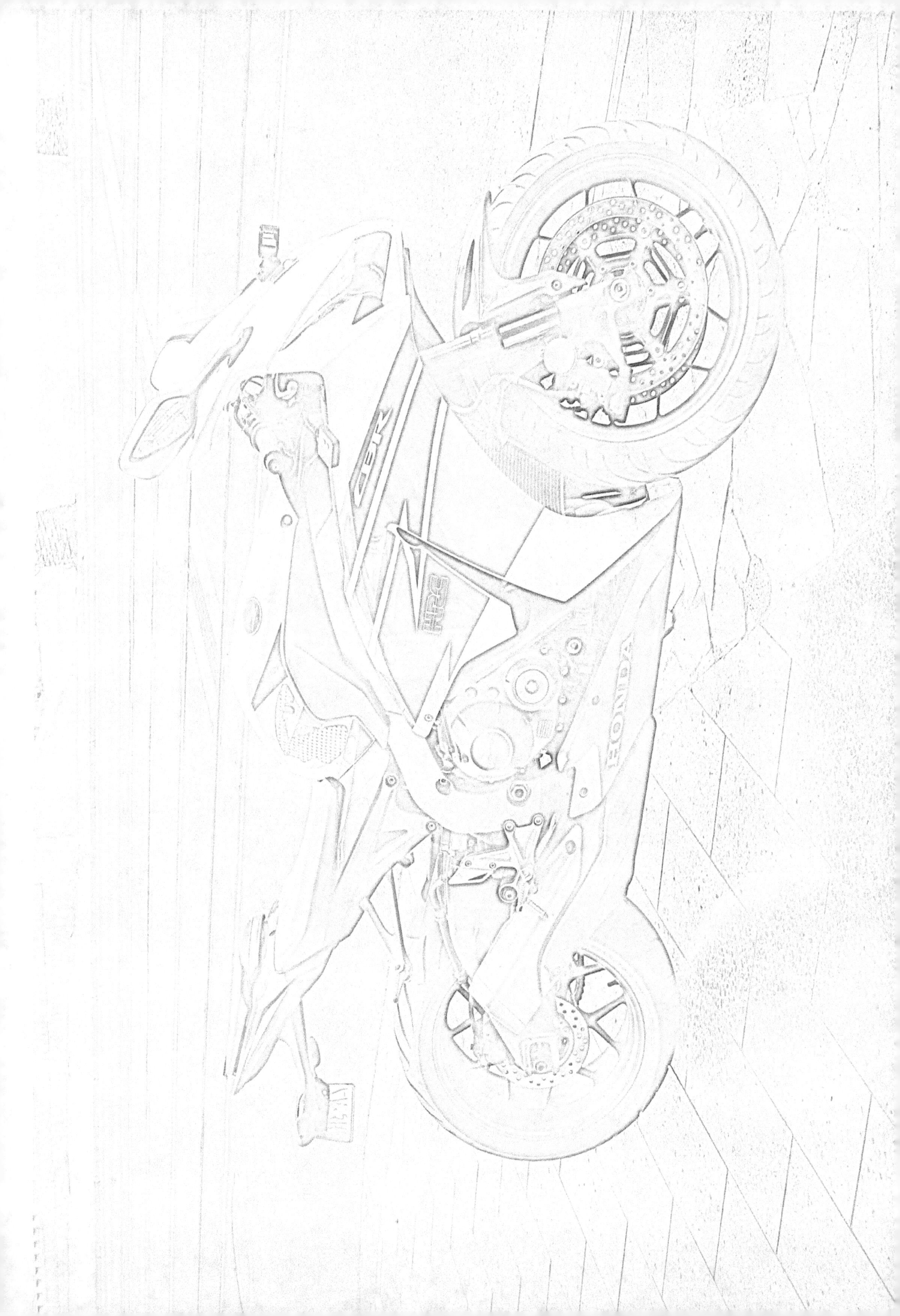
CBR
HRC
HONDA

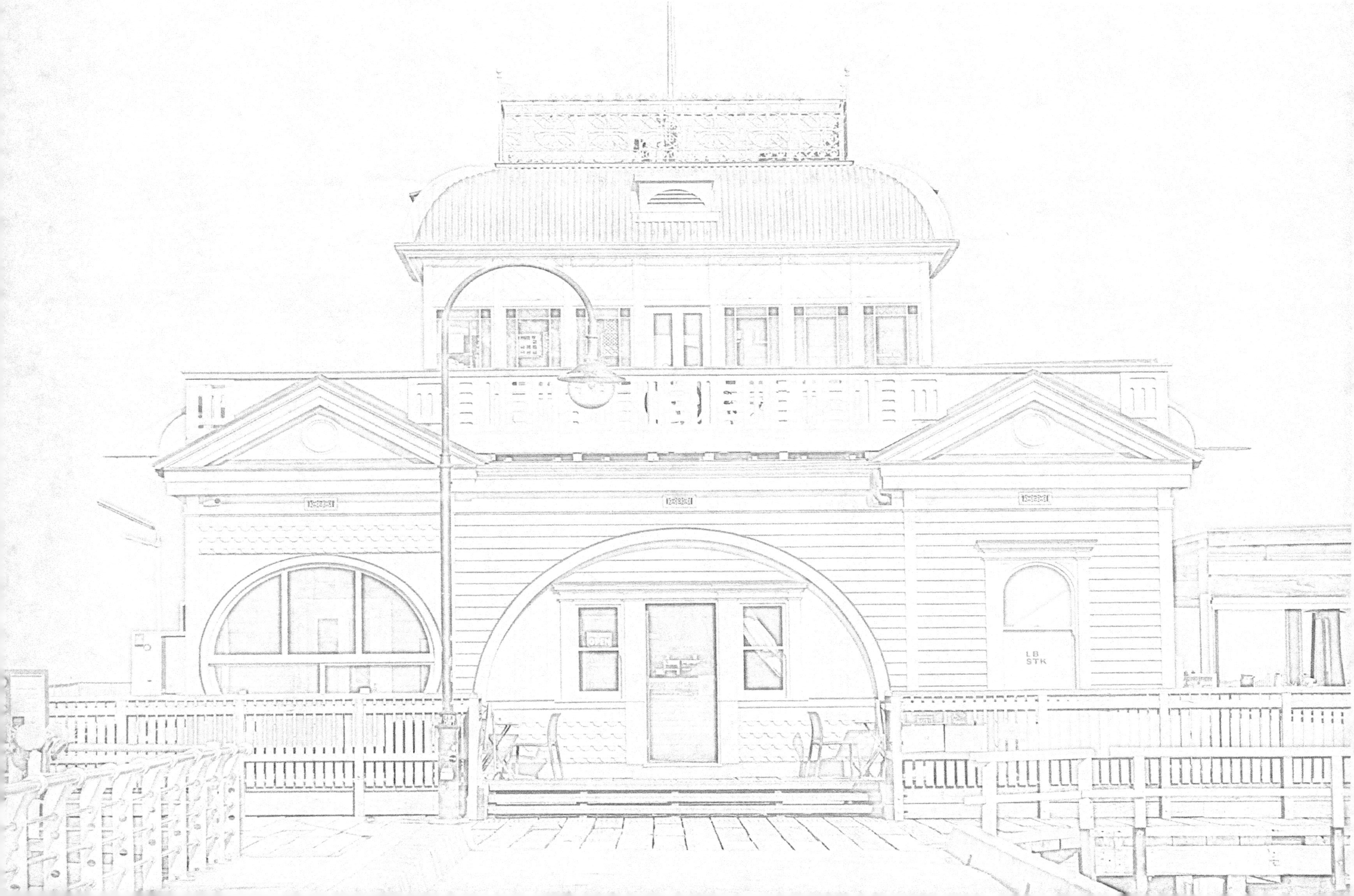
OPEN
LB
STK

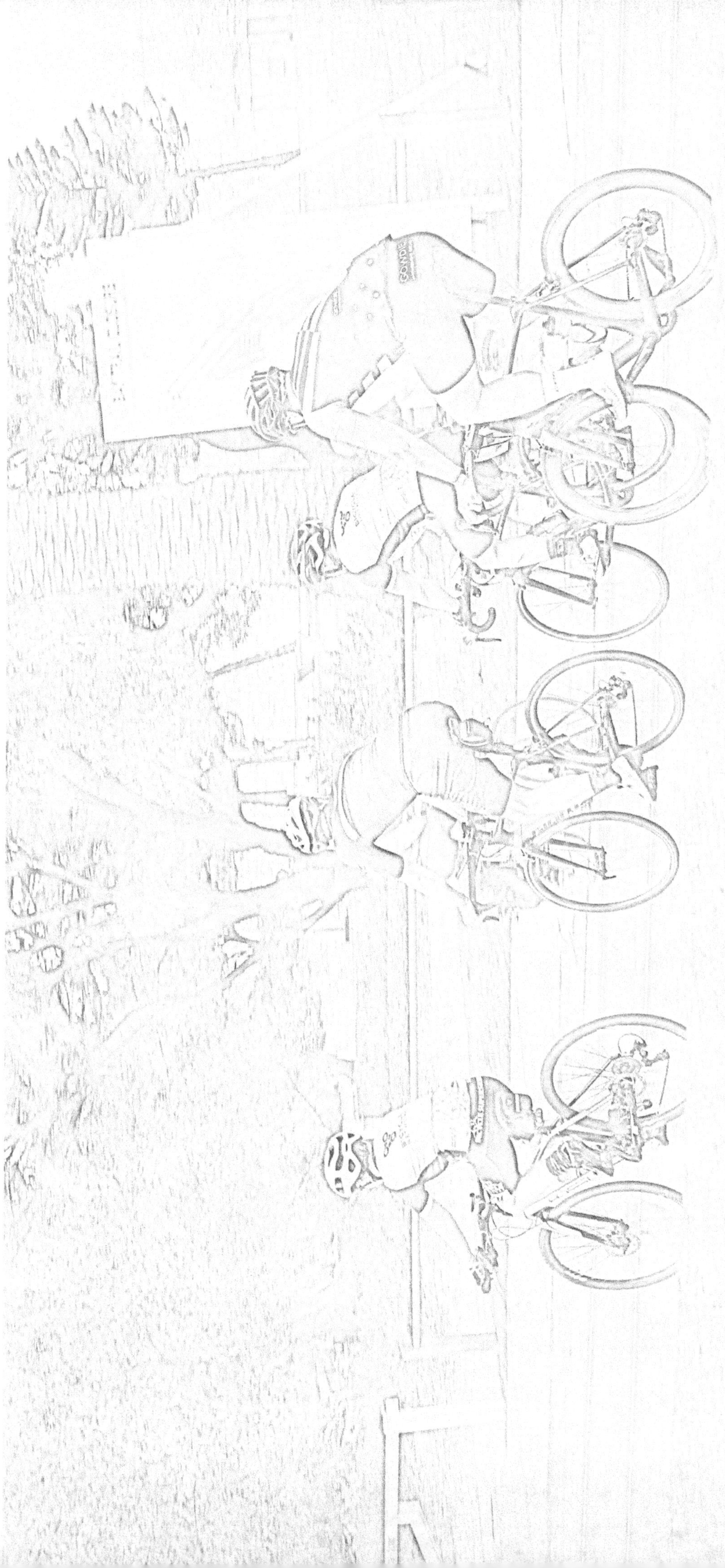

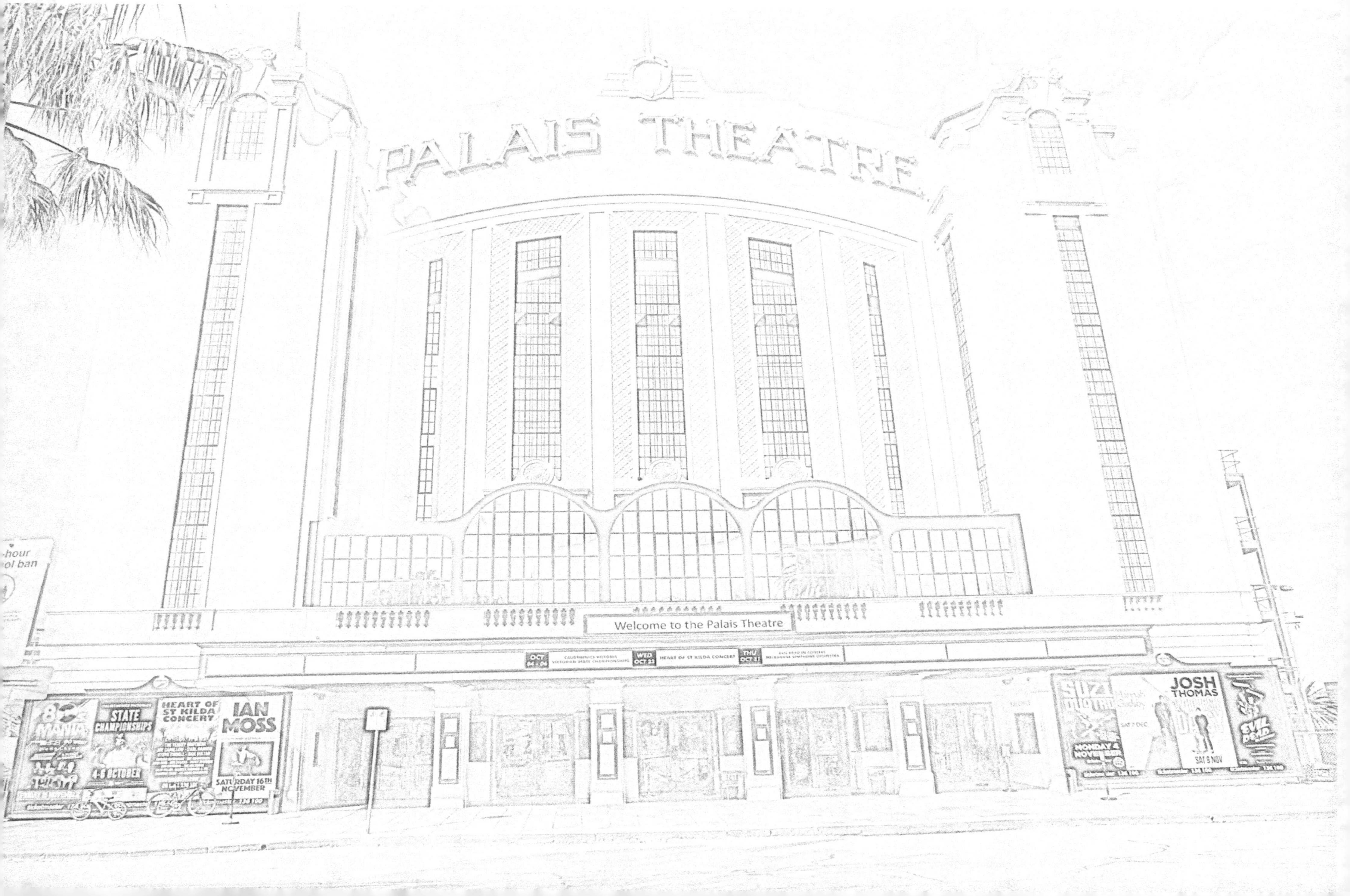
PALAIS THEATRE
Welcome to the Palais Theatre
HEART OF ST KILDA CONCERT
STATE CHAMPIONSHIPS
4-6 OCTOBER
IAN MOSS
SATURDAY 16TH NOVEMBER
JOSH THOMAS
SAT 9 NOV
SAT 7 DEC
EVIL DEAD

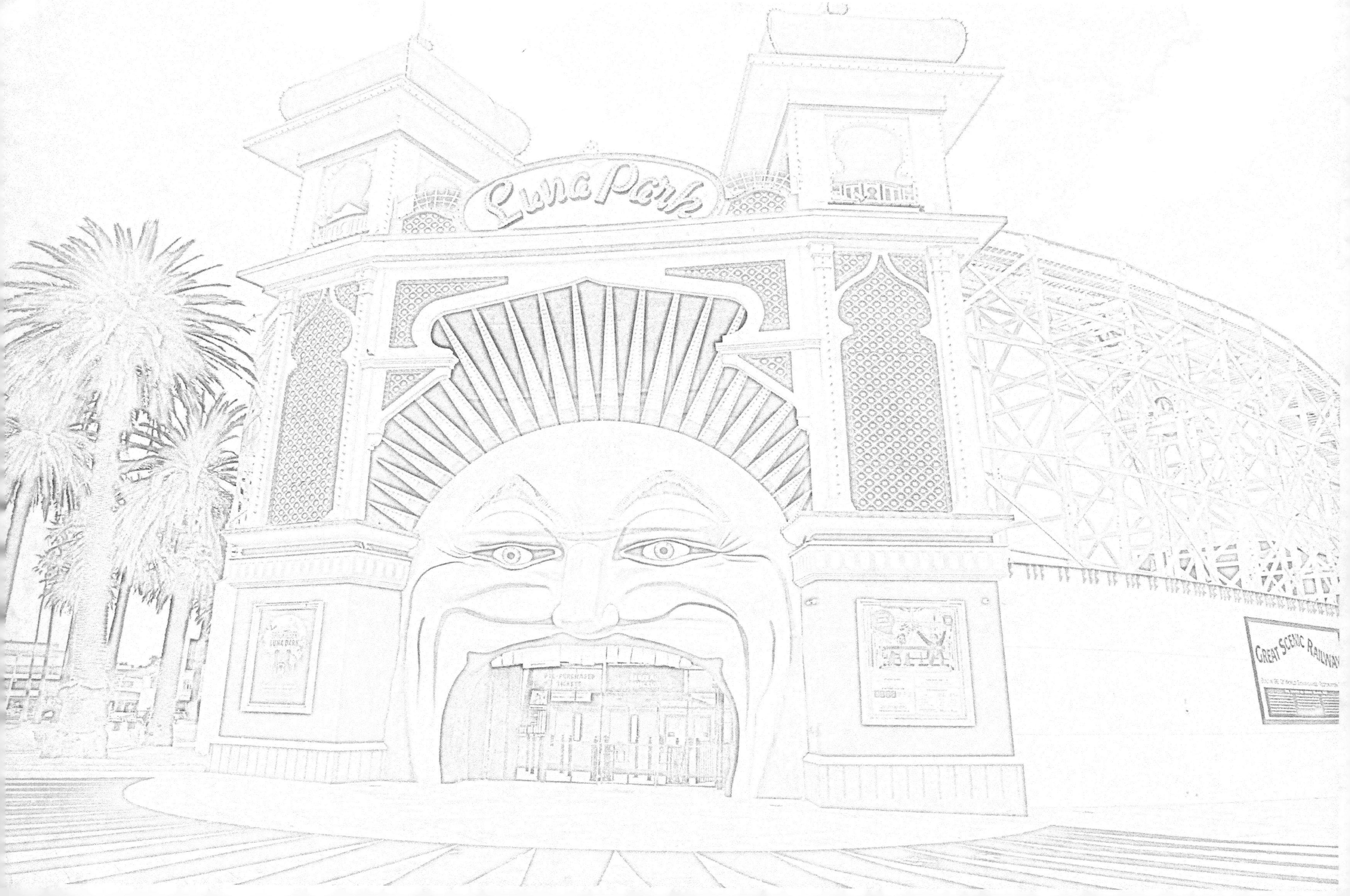
Luna Park
Great Scenic Railway

McDonald's
3504
Real friends.
Real friends.
3535

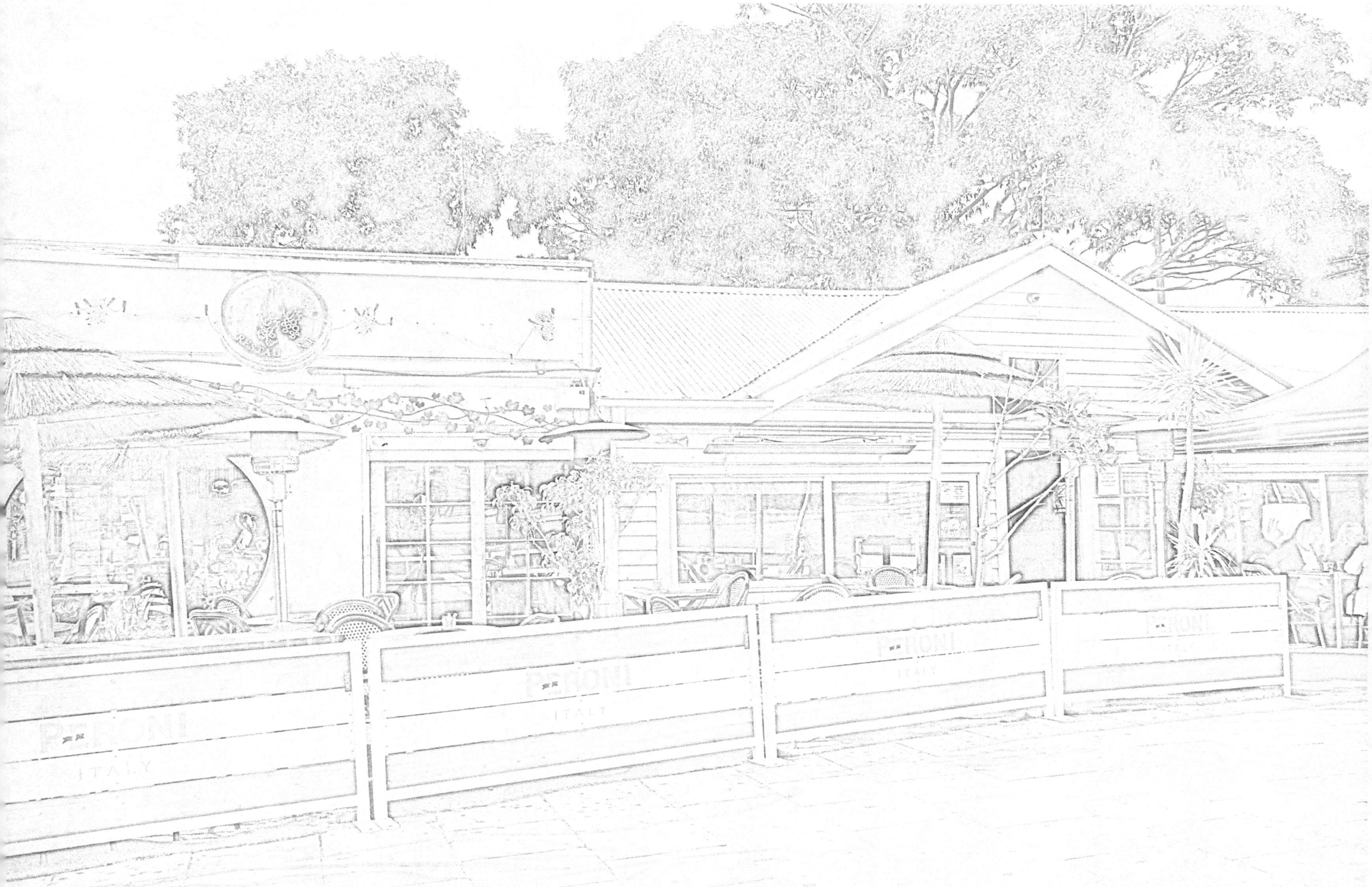

PERONI
ITALY
PERONI
ITALY
PERONI
ITALY

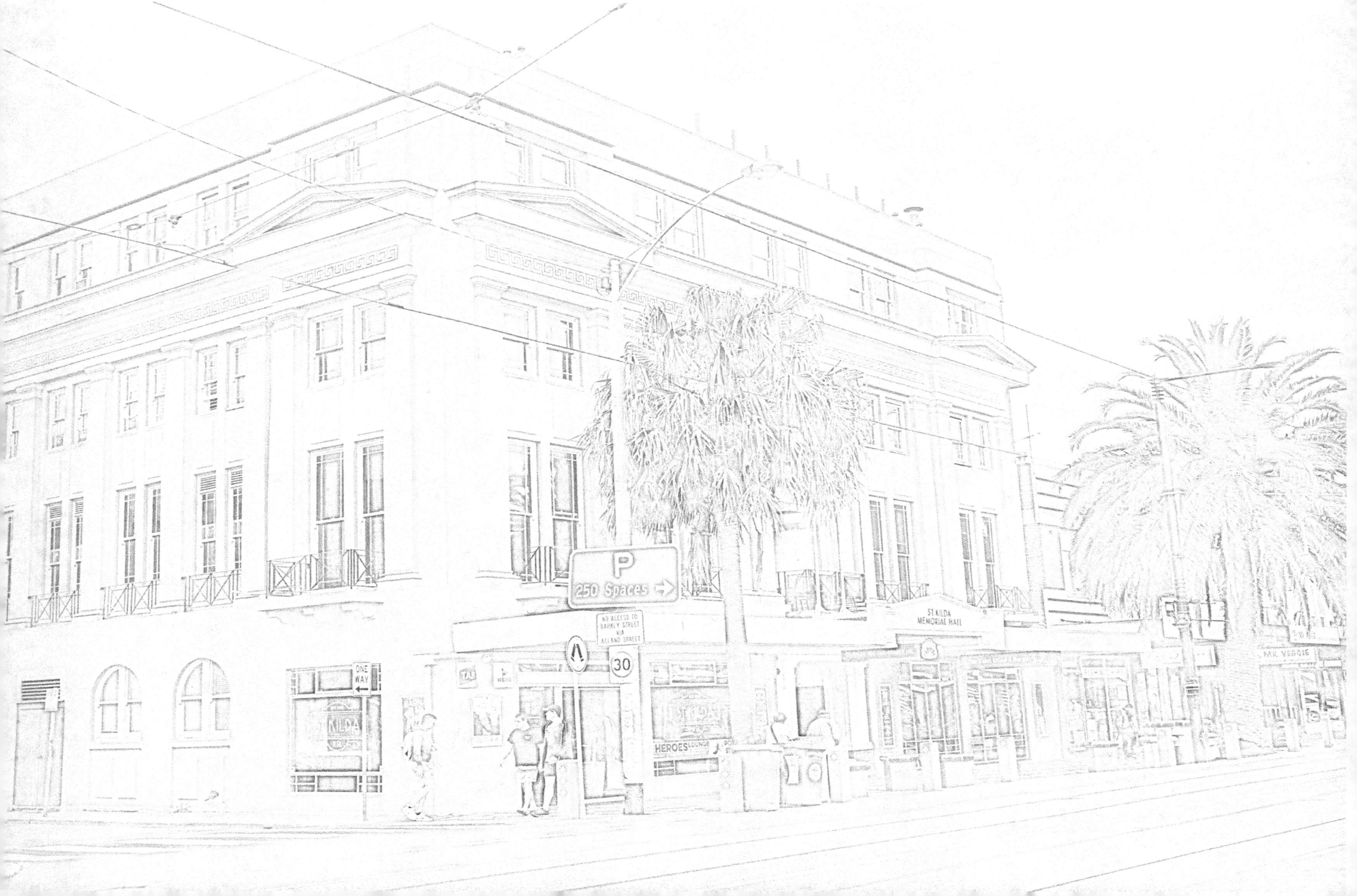
P
250 Spaces
NO ACCESS TO BARKLY STREET VIA ACLAND STREET
30
ONE WAY
ST.KILDA MEMORIAL HALL
HEROES LOUNGE
MR. VEGGIE

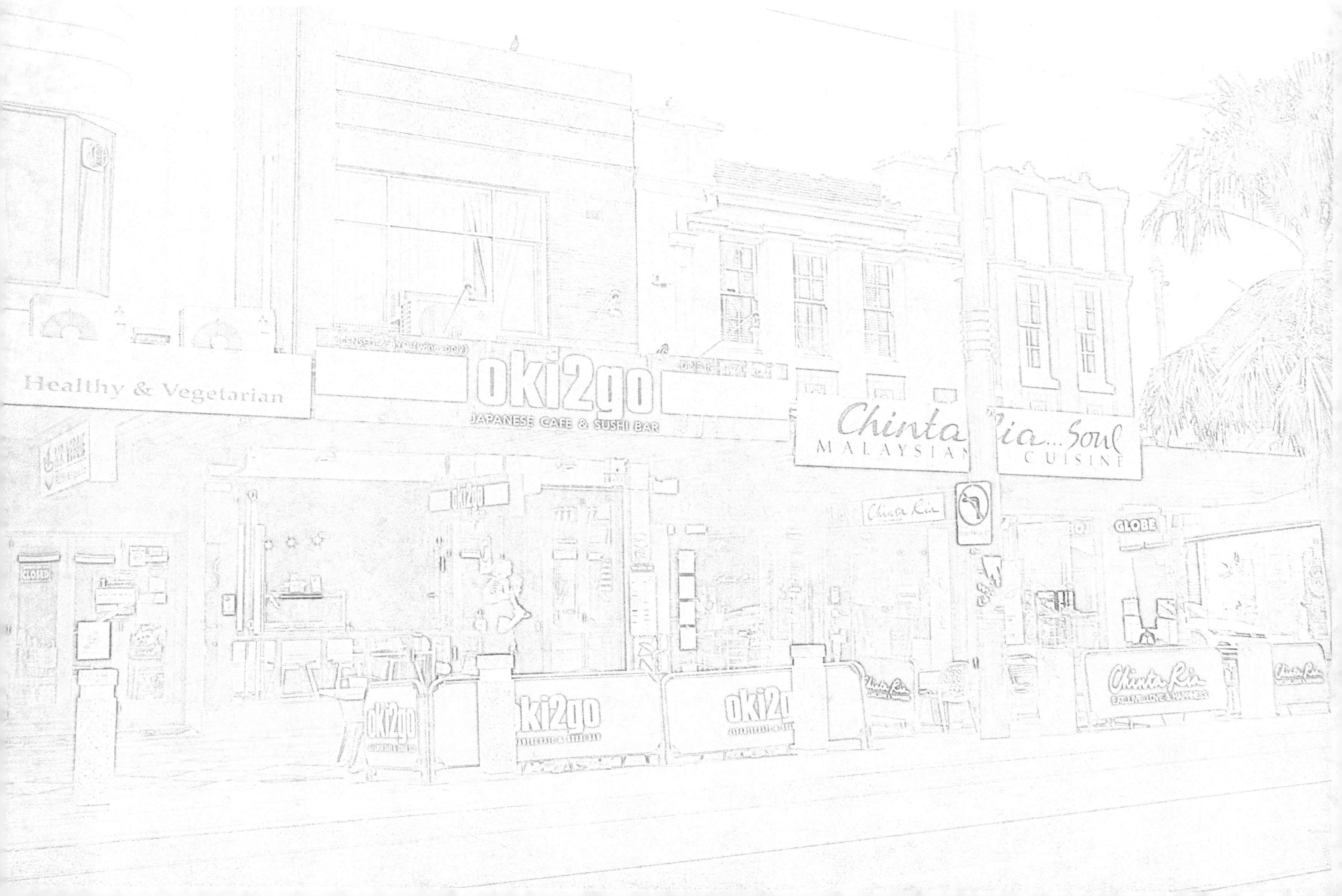
Healthy & Vegetarian
oki2go
JAPANESE CAFE & SUSHI BAR
Chinta Ria... Soul
MALAYSIAN CUISINE
Chinta Ria
GLOBE
CLOSED
Chinta Ria
EAT LIVE LOVE & HAPPINESS
oki2go
ki2go

www.ingramcontent.com/pod-product-compliance
Lightning Source LLC
Chambersburg PA
CBHW081100180526
45170CB00005B/1827
* 9 7 8 0 3 5 9 9 7 2 2 6 5 *